THE MASTER MAGICIANS

WALTER GIBSON

THE MASTER MAGICIANS

Their Lives
and
Most Famous Tricks

CITADEL PRESS   SECAUCUS, N.J.

Published by Citadel Press
A division of Lyle Stuart Inc.
120 Enterprise Ave., Secaucus, N.J. 07094
In Canada: Musson Book Company
A division of General Publishing Co. Limited
Don Mills, Ontario
Manufactured in the United States of America
ISBN O-8065-0921-X

ACKNOWLEDGMENTS

The author extends special acknowledgment and personal appreciation to the following friends who furnished valuable memorabilia and photographs from their collections, to illustrate the stories in this book:

Robert Lund; John Henry Grossman, M.D.; Irving Desfore; Morris O. Young, M.D.; Sidney Radner; Edgar Heyl; and David Price, who supplied rare material from his Egyptian Hall in Nashville, Tennessee.

To the memory of my friend
Fulton Oursler,
who always wanted me to write this book

BOSTON MUSEUM

MANAGER......................................Mr. R. M. FIELD

THE WONDER OF THE 19th CENTURY!

THE GREAT AND ONLY

HERRMANN

PREMIER OF ALL MAGICIANS.

FOR THREE NIGHTS

AND

One Matinee Only!

SPECIAL ATTENTION!

The Management has the honor of announcing to the public that the name Prof. HERRMANN having been established throughout the civilized World from 1856 with his elder brother, who, having retired from the profession leaves him in possession of the undisputed title of the GREATEST MAGICIAN OF THE WORLD, without an equal, and who has been proclaimed by the American and European Press the

Most Wonderful Prestidigitateur the World has ever Produced.

NO MACHINERY!
NO CONFEDERATES!
NO ELECTRICITY!

TWO AND A HALF HOURS OF UNALLOYED LEGERDEMAIN

By the Prince of Necromancers. The Only Magician who can keep his audience in a continuous roar of laughter and astonishment. Come and see for yourself. As he says, "the more you look, you never see nothing."

SPIRITUALISM EXPOSED

Prof. HERRMANN will also introduce for the first time in this City his Marvelous

SPIRITUAL MANIFESTATIONS

Which have created the most profound wonder and astonishment throughout the United States and Europe, introducing the Superlative Parisian Spirit Medium,

M'LLE ADDIE,

Who will positively appear at each entertainment in her

BEWILDERING SEANCES!

REMEMBER!

LADIES' and CHILDREN'S MATINEE
AND
ONLY MATINEE,
SATURDAY, July 8th

MONDAY, July 10th, THE SUMMER SEASON, and Production of the Famous American Opera Bouffe,

"EVANGELINE!"

With an UNEXAMPLED ARRAY OF TALENT.

PRICES.		
Orchestra.................$1.00	Admission.......................35 cents	
Balcony.................75 cents	Admission for Children under	
Parquet Circle.........50 cents	10 years of age...............15 cents	
Balcony Circle.........50 cents		
Evening Performance commence at 8 precisely...........Afternoon at 2 o'clock		

SEATS SECURED SIX DAYS IN ADVANCE by Mail or Telegraph.

F. A. Searle, Printer, 262 Washington Street, Boston.

One of Alexander Herrmann's American showbills, describing his full evening performance.

CONTENTS

INTRODUCTION

This is the story of the golden era of modern magic, told through the adventures of outstanding masters of the craft, whose careers formed an unbroken chain for more than a century. Choice has been made from the better-known magicians of each period, to stress the development of that particular phase.

By the early 1840s, magic had gradually but successfully emerged from the clutches of traveling mountebanks and showmen who worked their hanky-panky in the booths of outdoor fairs. It remained for a French conjuror, Robert-Houdin, to couple artistry with ingenious mechanical devices that gave mere tricks the dignity of magical experiments. His story, with his stress on elegance and refinement in conjuring, marks the first chapter of the golden era.

Of equal importance was Professor Anderson, who actually preceded Robert-Houdin as a performer, and continued on to greater exploits for fifteen years after Robert-Houdin's retirement. Anderson turned magic into a grand stage spectacle and raised it to the status of a dramatic presentation, a field in which he also excelled. Anderson, too, was the first magician to travel on a world-wide scale.

During the period of the three Herrmanns, Carl, Alexander and Leon, stage effects were developed into illusions, a term applied to the production, transformation and disappearance of living persons, or large animals or objects. Carl Herrmann, a contemporary of Robert-Houdin and Anderson, helped usher in that period, but it was Carl's youngest brother, Alexander, who first presented stage illusions on a grand scale.

Alexander was known in America both as the "Great Herrmann" and "Herrmann the Great." His untimely death in 1896 marked the mid-point of the golden era, and many connoisseurs of conjuring felt that the art had passed its peak, for to them, Herrmann the Great was the beau ideal of magic. A change was definitely in the making, for the rise of vaudeville and the lure of its big money induced younger magicians to develop specialty acts, ranging from sleight of hand to the brief presentation of a few large tricks and illusions.

Even Adelaide Herrmann, widow of Herrmann the Great, and Leon Herrmann, Alexander's nephew, went their separate ways in vaudeville, each with an individual act, attracting patrons by the magic of the name that stood for magic itself. But the full evening show continued to dominate the American stage. After Herrmann's death, his chief rival, Harry Kellar, continued to tour America with his own big show until his retirement a dozen years later.

Both Alexander Herrmann and Harry Kellar owed much of their success to a man named William Robinson, who had designed new and remarkable stage illusions first for Kellar, then for Herrmann. A capable magician in his own right, Robinson styled himself the "Man of Mystery," and he was to fulfill that title in a fabulous way. His double life in magic, his unfortunate but dramatic death, form a unique chapter in the modern saga of sorcery.

Howard Thurston, who began as a specialist in sleight of hand, became Kellar's successor and presented stage illusions on the grandest scale of all. Not content with merely vanishing people—as many as half a dozen at a time—he also caused lions, tigers, pianos, horses and even automobiles to come and go before the eyes of astonished onlookers. Thurston ranks high among the "greats," because his show, if not the best, was certainly the biggest ever seen in America.

Another remarkable chapter was provided by Houdini and his brother Hardeen, who early postponed their magical ambitions to become "escape kings," mysteriously extricating themselves from handcuffs, jails and whatever other restraints challengers might propose. For years, the public regarded Houdini more as a human enigma than a master magician, but toward the end of his career he blended his flare for showmanship with his conjuring skill in a full evening show which was unique in magical annals. Unfortunately, like the Great Herrmann, Houdini died too soon, and it remained for Hardeen to carry on their mutual tradition.

From the days of Anderson, the lure of far-offs lands had beckoned both European and American magicians. Occasionally, a magician took to travel in his early career, hoping to find untapped fields; while others, in later life, embarked on extensive tours to cash in on the fame that had spread ahead of them.

With the rapid expansion of steamship and railroad transportation in the early 1900s, it became possible to carry a full-sized magic show anywhere in the world, and the man who first turned this into a full-time opportunity was a young magician named Raymond. As a globe-trotter, he set the standard for a generation that was to follow, and wherever these newcomers went, they found the name of the Great Raymond established as a master of modern magic.

Raymond's chapter concludes the passing of the colorful century of conjuring, in which the exploits of representative master magicians have epitomized the careers of many others, equally deserving of a place in mystery's Hall of Fame.

elles font toujours fortement ferrées entre l'in-dex & le petit doigt d'une part, & les deux doigts du milieu qui font deffous. 5°. Déployez un peu le pouce pour lâcher le paquet fupérieur, en l'appuyant fur l'index & le petit doigt, & portez en même temps fur le pouce le paquet inférieur. Voyez la *fig. 30.*

Dans cette cinquième pofition, le paquet in-férieur a déjà pris le deffus, & les figures des cartes, dans les deux paquets, font tournées vers la terre. 6°. Otez le pouce d'entre les deux paquets pour le faire paffer deffus, en pouffant les deux paquets vers la naiffance du pouce, de manière qu'ils fe trouvent parfaitement l'un fur l'autre pour n'en faire qu'un, *fig. 31.*

Dans

A page from a book on magic written by Decremps in 1789, illustrating the "pass" with a pack of cards that Robert-Houdin practiced as a youth.

Chapter 1

ROBERT-HOUDIN

(1805–1871)

Early one evening in the mid-1820s, a bookseller named Bertrand was about to close his shop in the French town of Blois when a last-minute customer entered. Bertrand recognized the arrival as Jean Eugène Robert, a youth of about twenty, whose father was one of the best watchmakers in Blois. For weeks, Jean had been saving his money to buy two volumes on clockmaking by Ferdinand Berthoud, which the bookseller had put aside for him.

Bertrand brought the books down from a high shelf and wrapped them while Jean counted out the money. Soon Jean was hurrying homeward through narrow, winding streets, where houses with blue slate roofs and red brick chimneys rose high above the river Loire. He crossed the Rue Denis Papin, named in honor of a native of Blois, who had invented one of the earliest steam engines. Perhaps some day the town would also have a Rue Jean Eugène Robert, named after a great clockmaker-to-be.

Jean had been born in Blois on December 6, 1805, and had lived there until he was eleven years old. His father had then sent him to school at Orléans, thirty-five miles up the Loire. At eighteen, Jean had graduated and had returned to Blois, where his father wanted him to become a lawyer rather than a watchmaker.

Jean's penmanship was excellent, and he was immediately

accepted as a clerk in an attorney's office, but instead of studying law, he had spent his spare time devising mechanical gadgets. After about two years, his employer had sent him back to his father as better suited to the watchmaking trade. By then, Jean's father had retired, so he had become an apprentice in his cousin's shop. Now, eager to learn all he could regarding work he really liked, Jean had saved up for those volumes by Berthoud, intending to study them in detail.

But when Jean unwrapped the package in his upstairs room, he stared in utter surprise. The books were entitled *Scientific Amusements,* and they dealt, not with clockmaking, but with "Guessing a Person's Thoughts," performing "Tricks with Cards," "Restoring Dead Birds to Life" and a variety of subjects that became more fanciful the more deeply Jean delved into the pages.

The bookseller had mistakenly given Jean two volumes of a scientific encyclopedia, instead of the more staid work on horology. These particular volumes were compiled from such authors as Decremps, Guyot and Ozanam, who dealt with the subject of conjuring, or "white magic" as it then was termed.

To Jean, this was even more fascinating than clockmaking, and he was lost in a perusal of his new theme when his candle sputtered out. Sleep was out of the question. From his window he gazed longingly at a glowing street lamp that was suspended over the center of the thoroughfare from two side poles. It struck him that here was a way to put his newly gained knowledge of conjuring to practical use. So he started out with a pair of pliers in one hand, his hat in the other, intending to detach the lamp and spirit it back, lighted but unseen, to illuminate his room.

Hardly had he loosened the oil lamp and covered its flickery flame with his hat, before he saw a baker's helper coming from a nearby shop. Jean slid into a convenient doorway, only to be trapped there when the baker lounged outside the shop, calmly smoking his pipe and blocking Jean's return to his lodging. In the midst of this dilemma, the lining of Jean's hat caught fire and he was forced to extinguish it, lamp and all, rather than betray his presence. Then, chancing a moment when the man was glancing the other way, Jean managed to speed off down the street in the darkness. He reached his lodging safely by a long, roundabout route, but his first effort to perform a hat trick was a decided fizzle.

That, however, did not deter his new urge to become a conjuror. Week after week, Jean studied those fabulous volumes, putting all his spare time into practicing sleight of hand. He learned to make the pass with a pack of cards, whereby the two halves are transposed unseen, so that a selected card can be brought secretly from the center of the pack to the top. Though both hands were used in the more popular version of this sleight, young Jean acquired the one-hand method as well.

Thus, while eating soup, or writing with his right hand, his left could be busy with a pack of cards that was always handy in the pocket of his loose-fitting jacket, which was sufficiently ample for the one-hand pass yet just cramped enough to facilitate the sleight. While walking to and from work, Jean habitually kept both hands thrust deep in those big pockets, palming such objects as coins, corks, or lumps of sugar that he carried for the purpose.

Here, the budding wizard was forced to improvise, for the magical books of the period were hazy on the palming process. Often they spoke only of "concealing" a coin in one hand, or "cleverly" substituting an object for a duplicate. It was up to the reader to guess whether a coin should be palmed in the bend of the fingers, the fork of the thumb, or whether it should actually be pressed deep into the palm itself and retained there.

That, perhaps, was why so few people learned legerdemain from books in those days. But Jean Robert was a striking exception. A good student, with hands already skilled in watchmaking, he progressed rapidly with his conjuring, keeping that

3

interest strictly to himself rather than be criticized for wandering from his chosen trade.

At the same time, his work at the watchmaker's bench actually improved, for he was anxious to finish early and get back to his books and sleights. Also, his hands were acquiring new skill through practicing those manipulations, which made him more deft in repairing watches. Within a year, his apprenticeship was over, and he was given a job by a watchmaker named Noriet in Tours, thirty-five miles down the Loire.

That proved fortunate indeed. Monsieur Noriet was a capable sculptor and devoted most of his time to that work, leaving the watch repairs to Jean, who became practically a member of the family. What was more, Noriet expressed an admiration for all forms of artistry, and when Jean brought out his cards, coins and a set of cups and balls, he was soon invited to perform for the family circle. Nowhere else could he have found such an appreciative audience. In his spare time he was able to increase his repertoire, so that his brief performances were always new.

On Friday, July 25, 1828, Jean accompanied the Noriets to a fair, where they stayed late, giving him a chance to watch some jugglers and mountebanks perform a few indifferent tricks. When the family arrived home, the dinner had gone cold, so it was warmed over for them, and Jean ate heartily of a beef stew that the others found distasteful. That night he was stricken with ptomaine poisoning, which might have proven fatal but for the prompt efforts of the family physician. After long days of raging fever, Jean began to recover. However, he felt weak and despondent, and wanted to get back to Blois.

The doctor advised against travel, warning him that it might bring on a relapse, but when Jean awoke early one morning, feeling much better, he decided to start out for home without telling anyone. There were only a few passengers on the stagecoach, and Jean found a seat alone in the *rotonde*, or rear compartment. Soon, the horses were galloping on their way. For

Jean, the jouncing and swaying of the coach became unbearable. His fever returned with a maddening intensity, reaching such a burning pitch that in desperation he flung open the rear door and sprang out.

The stagecoach was traveling faster than he realized, and he was unable to break his fall. His head-splitting agony ended with a blow that left him unconscious. When he awoke, he found himself in a narrow bed that was not his own. It stood beside an oak-paneled wall in a room measuring about six by nine feet. Crimson curtains hung at the far end, and through windows in the side walls, Jean could see the landscape gliding by. From beyond the partition beside the bed came a man's voice, clucking to a team of horses.

All this was soon explained by a stranger who approached the bed and gave Jean a spoonful of medicine. The man was in his fifties and had the appearance of a doctor, with a solemn but kindly face, and long black hair that fell to his shoulders. He introduced himself as Signor Torrini and announced that this carriage was not only his home, but served him as a theater, for he was a conjuror by profession and beyond the crimson curtains was the stage where he set up his apparatus.

Torrini explained that he was on his way from Orléans to Angers and had been taking a morning walk beside the horses, when he had seen Jean lying in the road and had told his driver, Antonio, to halt the wagon. They had put Jean in the bed and during the days that the horses had plodded on toward Angers, Torrini, who had some knowledge of medicine, had nursed his chance patient through his fever turn.

Thus began an adventure that Jean Robert was always to remember. At Angers, he watched from the window of an inn while Torrini and Antonio transformed their wheeled home into a theater. They folded the furniture into the walls and ceiling, then removed the partition between the rooms. The wagon's length of nearly twenty feet was doubled when they

5

pulled out an inner section from its encasing shell, in the manner of a telescope.

The extension was supported by strong props and the result was a miniature auditorium. There seats were arranged to accommodate a few dozen spectators, who entered by a special flight of steps past a ticket window underneath an extended canopy.

The first night's audience was less than capacity, but it included Jean, who watched the performance in fascination. Due to the limitation of the stage and the intimacy of the audience, Torrini presented a program composed chiefly of card tricks, rather than effects requiring boxes with false bottoms, heavily draped tables deep enough to hide an assistant, or other cumbersome apparatus.

Jean had read descriptions of those appliances in conjuring books, and he knew that keen spectators would be suspicious of such timeworn devices. But Torrini's sleights were baffling even to Jean, though he had read and practiced all of them. He realized at intervals that Torrini must have executed the pass, secretly "changed" one card for another and even palmed cards from the pack and replaced them; but his moves were always delayed until moments when they were least expected, or when attention was diverted elsewhere.

As he watched this master manipulator, Jean was gaining lessons in two vital phases of the magician's art, timing and misdirection, which at that time were scarcely mentioned in any book, and could only be appreciated by first-hand observation. So intent was Jean upon the performance that he never realized he himself was under even closer observation by Torrini.

That came out after the show. When Torrini asked Jean if he had enjoyed it, Jean replied that it was the most marvelous performance he had ever witnessed. Torrini bowed at the compliment, observing that it was indeed flattering, coming from someone who already possessed some degree of conjuring skill.

The statement dumfounded Jean. Torrini had learned that he

was a watchmaker from identification papers he carried in his wallet; but in his feverish departure from Tours, Jean had left behind his conjuring books, his playing cards, and other articles that might have furnished a clue to his interest in magic.

Smiling at Jean's wonderment, Torrini explained that while he performed, he watched the reactions of his audience and governed his routine accordingly. The moment the curtain rose, he had noted that Jean looked like a gourmet sitting down to a tasty dinner. During tricks where Torrini drew attention one way, Jean had been slow to follow, preferring to keep his eyes on the right spot. Torrini thus recognized that Jean not only had a passion for magic, but was already versed in it.

Torrini insisted that Jean travel along with the show until he had fully recovered from his illness. When Jean hesitated, unwilling to impose upon his benefactor, Torrini brought out a box containing a miniature figure of a clown, which was supposed to jump into sight when the lid was opened, go through some gyrations and automatically return to the box.

The automaton was in such total disrepair that it practically had to be built over, and Torrini proposed that Jean, with his knowledge of clocks and watches, should undertake the task. To that Jean agreed, and went along with Torrini, setting up a workshop in the wagon.

While they traveled, Jean rebuilt the "Jumping Harlequin," as the automaton was called, and between times Torrini gave him constructive advice toward improving his sleights. In addition, Torrini revealed many of his own pet methods, including his "Piquet Trick," in which he allowed himself to be blindfolded, yet dealt a winning hand of cards from a pack shuffled by a spectator. During the rest of the summer, Jean also watched Torrini's performances in every town where they stopped and studied the reaction of the audiences.

Their route took them southward toward Bordeaux, but they turned eastward at Angoulême and continued through Limoges on their way to Clermont, where Torrini intended to conclude his season and return to Italy. Progress was slow, for they had only two horses pulling their huge, heavily constructed wagon, and they stopped in every town large enough to provide an audience for Torrini's miniature theater. Then as they were coming down a hill into the town of Aubusson, catastrophe struck.

Torrini was up front with Antonio, who was driving the horses, and Jean was in his mobile workshop, finishing his repairs on the automaton, when the wagon gave a sudden lurch. Jean realized that the brake had snapped on the rear wheels and no longer acted as a drag when Antonio hauled on the rope. But before Jean could reach the door, the vehicle was barreling down the hill, forcing Antonio to race the horses ahead of it to prevent it from overturning.

Remembering his unwise leap from the stagecoach, Jean decided to cling to his workbench and trust in Antonio, who was handling the horses well enough to regain control of the wagon when they reached the level road below. But before then, a huge haycart came from a side road between two houses, completely blocking the way as it tried to turn.

In the crash that followed, both of Torrini's horses were killed, the huge vehicle was overturned and much of its contents smashed. Torrini and Antonio were thrown clear, while Jean, inside the wagon, managed to brace himself and dodge the flying objects. Fortunately, the double construction of the wagon's frame and body saved it from demolition, and Jean was able to crawl from the wreckage, dazed but unhurt. He found Antonio cut and bruised, bending over Torrini, who had suffered a broken leg and dislocated shoulder from his long, hard fall to the road.

They took Torrini to an inn in Aubusson, where he began a slow but satisfactory recuperation from his painful injuries. Torrini had tended Jean through his illness; now Jean returned the favor. He set up his workshop in Torrini's bedroom and continued to rebuild the automaton, which had suffered further

8

damage in the crash. During the days that followed, Torrini related his life history, snatches of which Jean had already heard, but which now unfolded as a most amazing narrative, intermingling humor, pathos and stark tragedy.

According to Torrini, his real name was Edmond de Grisy, and he was the son of a French count who had been killed while defending his king during the bloody days of the Revolution. Edmond had escaped to Italy with enough money to study medicine in Florence and later become a practicing physician in Naples. There, during the Carnival of 1796, the public was excited over the performances of the celebrated Chevalier Pinetti, a professor of natural magic, who denied any power of sorcery, yet produced such mechanical marvels as a miniature orange tree on which, at his command, leaves, blossoms and finally fruit grew visibly before the eyes of the astonished onlookers. Actually, the branches were formed of hollow tubes, with leaves, blossoms and fruit made of silk, so they could be inflated with compressed air.

Another of Pinetti's favorite tricks was to burn a chosen playing card, pour the ashes into a gun barrel and fire at the wall of the stage, where the card reappeared, restored. This mystery depended on a special panel covered by a strip of cloth that could be whisked away to disclose the "restored" card, which until then was concealed beneath.

Pinetti varied the trick by borrowing a ring and firing it from a pistol at a casket, from which a dove appeared, carrying the ring in its beak. In this case, the ring was switched for a duplicate, and while Pinetti was loading the pistol, an assistant pushed the dove and the original ring through an opening in the scenery and up into a false-bottomed casket that was standing on a draped table.

Jean had read explanations of these tricks in his conjuring books, but it was interesting to hear the details from Torrini, who—as young Edmond de Grisy—had watched Pinetti perform them night after night, until he guessed most of the methods and began duplicating Pinetti's show to amaze and amuse his own friends. Word of this reached Pinetti, who called on Edmond, complimented his skill and offered to sponsor him in a public performance before the King of Naples.

Foolishly, Edmond agreed. The great night came, and almost from the start, one trick after another went wrong. Jeered and hissed by the audience, Edmond rang down the curtain and fled from the theater in despair. The next day, he learned that Pinetti had put in a prompt appearance and had taken over the stage, finishing the show in his usual skillful style. The failure of Edmond's tricks had all been arranged by Pinetti, as the most effective way to dispose of an unwanted rival.

Edmond gave up his medical practice and left Naples. His overwhelming desire was revenge, so he spent his fortune preparing a show to outdo Pinetti's and went on the road as a professional conjuror in his own right. Wherever possible, he crossed Pinetti's route and, by putting on a more elegant performance, featuring many novelties, Edmond drove Pinetti into obscurity and captured the field for himself.

During his travels, Edmond met and married a girl named Antonia Torrini. They had one son, Giovanni, who at the age of sixteen was working in the show. In one trick, Edmond fired a pistol at Giovanni, who was holding an apple between his teeth, and the bullet was found in the core of the apple. One night the trick failed and Giovanni was killed.

Edmond was imprisoned for six months on a charge of homicide through negligence, and during that period, Antonia died. Her brother Antonio urged Edmond to adopt the name of Torrini and start out again with his show. They had put all their money into building their traveling theater and Edmond had been performing as Torrini for two years when he came across Jean Robert lying in the road.

Possibly Torrini's claim of noble parentage was false, and he may have exaggerated his rivalry with Pinetti to increase his own prestige, for conjurors then—as now—thrived on self-

esteem and each liked to fancy himself as the world's greatest. Antonio, however, confirmed much of Torrini's later story,
including the fact that their entire savings had gone into the
theatrical wagon. With Torrini hospitalized, Antonio wondered
how they could raise the money needed to repair the vehicle
and obtain another pair of horses.

Young Jean Robert had a remedy for that. He had finished
fixing the automaton and to put the rest of Torrini's apparatus
in shape would take little time. So Jean went to the mayor's
home and proposed giving a magical performance for Torrini's
benefit. Jean demonstrated some of his own tricks for the
mayor's friends and they became enthusiastic over the idea.
A hall was furnished free of charge and enough tickets were
sold to fill it.

When Jean faced that capacity audience, he promptly went
into his card tricks, feeling sure of them. They were well received and he then turned to some of Torrini's own appliances.
He had often seen the master use them, but he felt shaky
as he presented them for the first time, even though Antonio
was standing in the wing as a ready assistant.

In one effect, the "Pyramids of Egypt," Jean showed two
goblets, one filled with water, the other with wine. He poured
both into a decanter which stood on a small pedestal and
called attention to the fact that the liquids were well mixed.
He then covered the decanter with an ornamental metal cone
and placed the empty goblets on side stands, covering them
with similar cones, as he proclaimed: "Behold! The Pyramids
of Egypt!"

Jean then ran a red ribbon from the central pyramid to the
one on the right, and a white ribbon to the one on the left. He
waved his hand above the red ribbon, and commanded the
wine to flow; then he did the same with the white ribbon,
commanding the water to flow. He kept repeating these ges-
tures, and as he did, he had the nervous urge to hurry through
the trick, but when he glanced toward the wing, he saw

Antonio spread his hands in warning, meaning, "Wait!" So Jean kept spreading his own hands to encourage the invisible flow, until he caught Antonio's nod. Then, lifting the enchanted pyramids, he showed a result that brought awed exclamations from the audience.

The decanter was totally empty, while each goblet now held its original contents, wine on the right, water on the left! Miraculously, Jean had caused the liquids to separate and travel along the ribbons to their proper destinations. As the audience broke into applause, Jean smiled away his worry. He was glad the trick was over, for from his standpoint it wasn't quite the miracle it seemed.

The decanter had a hole in the bottom, enabling the mixed liquids to pour down into the pedestal, which was hollow. But the flow, though steady, was so slow that Jean had ample time to cover the decanter before the decrease was noticeable. That flow continued while Jean was setting the goblets on the side stands and covering them with individual cones.

Each of those cones had a secret compartment in the top, containing just enough liquid to fill the glass. Each compartment had an outlet, but the liquid would not flow until air was admitted through an outer hole at the top. The air holes were plugged with a dab of wax that Jean thumbed away while placing the cones in position, letting each liquid flow down into its proper goblet.

Simple enough, if there was no slip. But Jean had wondered if he had removed the wax; he had listened for the liquid's trickle; he had even worried whether he had run each ribbon to its proper cone. Eager for the trick to finish, he would have lifted the cones too soon, but Antonio's warning had restrained him.

Jean felt safer when he came to the "Omelet Trick." This was sure-fire, in the full sense of the term. Jean borrowed a hat from a spectator and set it on a table, brim down, while he stepped aside, found a candle and lighted it. Then he placed the candlestick on the table in front of the hat.

This was all byplay to help what followed. On a shelf called a *servante*, behind the heavily draped table, was a metal cylinder with a dividing partition in its center. In the upper section was an omelet, already fully cooked; the lower half was empty. After lighting the candle, Jean picked up the hat, drew it toward him and tipped it forward, brim upward.

During that simple, natural action, done with his left hand, he reached behind the table with his right and loaded the cylinder into the hat, where it remained unseen. In the process, the cylinder was inverted, so that the end containing the omelet was downward; the empty section, upward. The audience, of course, knew nothing of that; they did not even suspect what had happened.

Now Jean waved to Antonio, who brought him a deep saucepan, along with a plate of eggs. Jean broke the eggs, poured them into the pan, and threw in the shells with them. Antonio brought salt, pepper and milk, which Jean added in profusion, along with a cup of flour. He stirred the mixture and poured it all into the hat, while the audience gasped a profound, "Ahhhh!"

Of course, it all went into the upper half of the double cylinder, though the audience supposed that the hat itself was receiving the ingredients. To confirm that notion, Jean lowered the mouth of the saucepan down into the hat, as though to dispose of the last drop. In doing so, he jammed the bowl-shaped pan over the hidden cylinder and brought both out as one, letting the omelet drop from the lower half and remain in the hat.

With that, the trick was already done. Jean handed the inverted saucepan to Antonio, who was standing by, and then held the hat over the candle flame, announcing to the audience that he intended to cook its contents. All that remained was to

13

tell a few stock jokes until Antonio returned with a plate on which Jean could dump the omelet.

But without realizing it, Jean lowered the hat too close to the candle flame. The audience laughed so loudly that he failed to hear Antonio's warning call. Too late, Jean realized that he had scorched and burned the outside of the hat. By moving the hat about, he finally extinguished the flame, but in so doing, smeared the hat with candle grease.

The audience was laughing at Jean, not with him, when Antonio arrived with the plate and undertoned, "Go right on." So Jean tilted the hat and showed the omelet, letting it fall onto the plate. Antonio took the hat and left the stage while Jean was exhibiting the result of his magical cookery; but soon, Antonio was back, bringing Jean's own hat, which closely resembled the one that Jean had borrowed and ruined. Pointing into it, Antonio called Jean's attention to a hastily scrawled note:

SORRY I BURNED YOUR HAT. PRETEND THIS ONE IS YOURS. SEE ME TOMORROW AND I WILL BUY YOU A NEW HAT.

Jean copied Antonio's pointing gesture when he returned the hat to his victim. The man saw the note and smiled, so the trick was a success. Jean then demonstrated the "Jumping Harlequin," which went through its surprising gyrations; and for a climax, he presented Torrini's blindfold piquet deal, which won the audience completely. Jean bowed off, happy and satisfied at the result of his first professional show, which he felt would be his last. He was now aware that it would require years of experience to gain a true command of the conjuror's art. Great though his urge in that direction, he felt that he belonged back in the watchmaker's trade.

The next day, Jean turned over most of the receipts to Torrini, who was overwhelmed with happy surprise. There was enough money for Torrini to pay off all his bills in Aubusson and buy a new team of horses besides. Jean kept only an amount sufficient to pay for the ruined hat and his stagecoach fare back to Blois.

In Blois, Jean worked for nearly two years in a watchmaker's shop, practicing his sleights in his spare time. To relieve the monotony, he joined an amateur theatrical company which presented popular plays of the day. During this period Jean met Josèphe Cécile Houdin, whose father—like Jean's—was a famous Blois watchmaker. They were married on July 8, 1830, and moved to Paris, where Jean's father-in-law had opened a wholesale clock business. There Jean set up a special department for the manufacture and display of mechanical toys and automatic figures.

To celebrate his marriage, Jean added his wife's name to his own, and officially became Jean Eugène Robert-Houdin. Jean's new friends called him Robert, and soon his name was known to many of the amateur conjurors in Paris, for like the rest, he frequented a little shop on the Rue Richelieu where magical appliances were sold.

From Papa Rujol, the elderly proprietor, Robert learned the details of many mechanical marvels, together with their improvements. With his own mechanical bent, Robert was particularly interested in automata of types more intricate than the "Jumping Harlequin." He was progressing in this field when he was asked to repair an immense contrivance called the Componium, a complete mechanical orchestra, which could play innumerable operatic airs with faithful exactitude, when in working order.

The Componium was far from that, when its parts were brought to Robert-Houdin's workshop in dozens of boxes and dumped there, in utter confusion. Much of the mechanism was rusted and broken, and before beginning his task, Robert was forced to study the operation of mechanical musical instruments with which he was unfamiliar. Starting almost from nothing, he assembled parts as one would the pieces of a patchwork puzzle. As the job progressed, his mind became so filled with it that the project grew to an obsession.

It took more than a year to complete the work. The final stages were most grueling of all, for time and again, a single slip might have brought failure. When the Componium was at last in working order, Robert suffered a nervous collapse and was stricken with a fever that left him delirious.

With his recovery, Robert lost all interest in everything about him. For nearly five years, even his attraction to conjuring and mechanical devices was gone, except as occasional recollections. At last he left Paris, and after six months in the country, he returned with his mind so cleared that he resumed work eagerly.

Robert's new mechanical toys were an immediate success. Among them was a magical clock which he constructed in duplicate and which created a sensation in the shop windows where it was displayed. The clock had a glass dial, supported upright on a glass pillar, both completely transparent. Yet the hands on the dial kept perfect time!

The secret was quite ingenious. The dial was actually double, consisting of two glass disks that appeared as one. The markings of the minutes and hours were inscribed upon one section of the dial, which was stationary. The other portion revolved, but the motion was invisible, being glass against glass. The hands were actuated by the revolution of the movable disk.

Anyone guessing that would still wonder what made the dial move, and the answer to that was equally clever. The glass column was hollow and within it was a glass rod turned by a mechanism in the stand on which the column was mounted. The rotation of the rod could not be seen, as it was glass within glass, and the upper end of the rod was geared to the rim of the movable dial, causing it to revolve.

Robert-Houdin also constructed mechanical figures of singing birds, an automatic figure of a dancer on a tightrope, and a miniature conjuror performing a trick with cups and balls. As his fame increased, he embarked on the project of a remarkable automaton that could write words and draw pictures. To avoid the strain he had experienced while repairing the Componium, Robert took a secluded workshop in a suburb of Paris and spent most of his time there.

More than a year passed before the automaton was successfully completed and Robert-Houdin was back in his old shop, making a steady profit from the sale of his mechanical devices. His fortunes seemed definitely on the upturn, when sudden tragedy struck. His wife died in October, 1843, leaving him with three young children.

His work, coupled with the care of the family, proved very taxing during the months that followed, but he managed to arrange a display of his automata at the exposition held in Paris in 1844. There his writing-and-drawing figure won the admiration of King Louis Philippe, and was bought by the famous American showman, Phineas T. Barnum, for his museum of curiosities in New York.

In August of that same year, Robert-Houdin married Marguerite Braconnier, a woman ten years younger than himself. His profit from the sale of his automata and the care that his new wife devoted to his children gave him both time and money to plan new projects.

While living in Paris, Robert had witnessed the performances of such noted magicians as Comte and Bosco, along with others of lesser fame. At Papa Rujol's, he had met a performer named Jules de Rovere, whose skill at sleight of hand was coupled with a desire for elegance. Rovere disliked the term *escamoteur* as applied to a conjuror, because it also signified a sharper. Nor did he care to be classed as a *physicien*, or professor of natural science, because it was too pretentious.

Therefore Rovere coined the word *prestidigitateur*, meaning a man skilled with his fingers, and later the term *prestidigitation*, referring to conjuring or magic itself. From these were derived the English word "prestidigitator," which is still in wide use today. While Robert-Houdin felt that such phraseology was on the pompous side, he admired Rovere's effort to add prestige to the art.

So, apparently, did a performer named Philippe, who arrived in Paris in 1841, and presented a remarkable performance in a specially built theater which he named the *Palais des Prestiges*, mingling prestige with prestidigitation. Robert-Houdin attended Philippe's show and was highly impressed by it.

When the curtain rose, the stage was totally dark, and a man in evening clothes, apparently the theater manager, came down the aisle to make an announcement to the audience. However, the man proved to be Philippe himself. Apologetically, he explained that he had been delayed in getting to the theater, but would make up for lost time by a trifling bit of magic.

With that, Philippe fired a huge pistol at the blacked-out stage. Instantly, hundreds of candle flames were lighted, dazzling the spectators with their brilliance. The stage was already set with Philippe's apparatus, so he went into a regular routine of card tricks, flower productions, and finally, the transformation of a vase full of coffee beans into fully brewed coffee, which was served to the audience.

Robert was intrigued by the "Candle Trick," as it involved electricity, which was very puzzling at that time. When Philippe aimed his gun, an assistant turned on a flow of hydrogen gas that escaped through tiny jets in the decorations behind each candle wick. At the gunshot, an electric current was sent through thin wires extending from tiny insulators, with sufficient gaps for a spark to jump at each wick, so the wicks caught fire when the sparks ignited the gas.

During the first act, Philippe also displayed several interesting automata. One was a figure of a juggler in Cossack costume, another a mechanical peacock which spread its tail and ate from its master's hand, while the last was a harlequin like the one Robert had repaired for Torrini.

After an intermission, the curtain rose on a dazzling scene of golden curtains and imitation jewels that fairly blazed in the glare of five hundred candles. This extravaganza was called "A Night in the Palace of Peking" and Philippe entered wearing a fantastic costume that was part Chinese and at the same time a throwback to the attire of the medieval necromancers. His gorgeous Oriental robe was adorned with cabalistic signs and he wore a tall, pointed hat surmounted by a crescent that could very well have been borrowed from a Chinese court astrologer.

Indeed, Philippe's opening trick was actually of Chinese origin. It employed a dozen heavy rings, perhaps ten inches in diameter, that linked and unlinked as he handled them, forming a silvery chain that was a striking contrast to the golden stage set. As a climax, Philippe blew upon the glittering rings as he jangled them and they separated magically, each proving its solidity with a resounding clang as it struck the stage and bounced there.

This was the first Parisian showing of the famous "Linking Ring Trick," which Philippe had learned from a troupe of Chinese wizards in Dublin a few years before. Today it is performed by magicians everywhere, and in skilled hands it still provides the same mystifying charm.

As another striking effect, Philippe borrowed a dozen handkerchiefs, rammed them into an old-style blunderbuss and fired it at a huge loaf of sugar, which was a very common article at that time. So solid was the sugar loaf that Philippe's comedy assistant, Domingo, had to bring an ax to chop it open. And behold! from the interior came those very handkerchiefs, which Philippe returned to the owners!

From a borrowed hat, Philippe produced enough huge colored plumes to make a feather bed, along with a variety of other objects. He suspended a great caldron from a tripod, filled it with water, dead pigeons and vegetables, then lighted a fire beneath it. Live pigeons promptly flew from the caldron, which was then shown completely empty.

For a finale, Philippe stood on a low isolated platform and produced several bowls of goldfish from a shawl, following that with productions of rabbits, ducks and chickens in the same manner. This, too, was a trick that Philippe had learned from the Chinese conjurors.

Philippe's commodious robe provided concealment for many articles, but its Chinese motif caused most people to minimize the importance of the costume. They also overlooked his heavily draped tables, which had to be massive to support so many candlesticks, and seemingly were designed merely to enrich the Oriental scene.

In his modest shop in the Marais quarter of Paris, Robert-Houdin paused frequently in his work to muse on the surprising trends that conjuring had taken. Rovere had gained agreement from the French Academy that the art deserved its own title of "prestidigitation." In contrast, Philippe had captivated the public by reverting to the panoply of a sorcerer, which his predecessors had avoided, fearing they would be accused of a league with the devil.

If only someone could combine those elements, building the skill of the artist up to the miraculous by discarding the trappings of the charlatan! With this in mind, Robert began designing glass apparatus that would be free from suspicion, and would replace cumbersome boxes that were obviously double-bottomed. He pictured a stage set as elegant as a drawing room, which would contain only undraped tables. His lighting would be gas, not candles, while his attire would be conventional evening dress.

Among Robert's patrons was the Count de l'Escalopier, who lived in a magnificent mansion on the Place des Voges. Robert had sold the Count one of his magical clocks, and had frequently given impromptu conjuring performances in the Count's home. One day, Robert-Houdin detailed his plans to the Count, who was so intrigued that he wanted to supply the funds to build the theater and its equipment at once. But Robert-Houdin declined the offer, rather than impose upon so generous a friend. That almost created a rift between them, and it was a few months before the Count de l'Escalopier visited the shop again, to ask a favor which he felt only Robert-Houdin could fulfill.

The Count explained that for nearly a year, sums of money had been disappearing from his desk. He had sent away the servants, one by one, hoping to detect the culprit. Instead, the thefts had increased and the Count was fearful that if a member of his family should catch the thief in the act, he might be desperate enough to commit murder to cover his escape. So the Count wanted Robert-Houdin to provide a secret device that would trap the guilty party.

Overnight, Robert-Houdin and two of his mechanics worked on such a contrivance. The next day, Robert-Houdin went to the Count's home while the servants were away, and installed the device in the desk. He then called in the Count, saying he was ready. On his right hand, Robert-Houdin was wearing a thickly padded glove. He used that hand to unlock the desk and slowly raise the lid.

Suddenly there was a pistol shot, and a thin steel rod snapped into sight with triphammer speed, only to disappear when the desk lid fell, leaving a curl of bluish smoke from the gun muzzle. As though completing one of his conjuring tricks, Robert-Houdin raised his hand for the Count to see. To the Count's amazement, the glove now bore the inked imprint of the word *Voleur*, meaning "Thief."

The contrivance was remarkable. A trifling lift of the desk lid released a spring that fired the pistol as an alarm and actuated an implement composed of tattoo needles, perfectly placed to brand the thief's hand before he could pull it away. The Count approved all but the last feature; fearful that the wrong person might open the desk, he suggested that it be modified. So instead of the branding needles, Robert attached a metal cat's claw, capable of delivering only a superficial scratch.

Two weeks passed. The Count de l'Escalopier paid daily visits to the watchmaker's shop but had nothing to report. Whether the thief suspected a trap or was temporarily content with his last big haul remained a question until one morning when the Count heard a gunshot. He raced from the library to his bedroom and encountered his most trusted servant, Bernard, who pointed out the way that the thief had gone. But as they took up the chase, they came to a locked door with the key in the lock. Obviously, no one could have gone out that way.

Swept by sudden suspicion, the Count turned and saw that Bernard was keeping his right hand behind him. Quickly, the Count snatched it into sight and saw the telltale claw scratch. Bernard broke down and admitted that he was the thief of the past two years. He had hoarded most of the money; to escape prosecution, he signed a full confession and returned fifteen thousand francs to his master.

Soon afterward, the Count called at Robert-Houdin's shop and told him how the thief trap had worked. Since the Count had recovered fifteen thousand francs through his friend's ingenuity, he insisted that Robert-Houdin accept a loan of that amount, to be used toward the construction of the magic theater and to be paid off from the profits gained from performances held there.

Under the circumstances, Robert-Houdin could no longer refuse. He took a suite of rooms above the archways surrounding the gardens of the Palais Royal, originally the residence of the famous Cardinal Richelieu. There, on Thursday, July 3, 1845, Jean Eugène Robert-Houdin presented the first of his *Soirées Fantastiques*, evenings of true enchantment that were to captivate Parisian audiences in the years to come.

Yet the opening performance had a dismal side. Although

a perfectionist in skill and technique, Robert-Houdin still needed the flair of the showman. That was not surprising, considering that this was only his second professional appearance, a long-delayed sequel to his debut in Aubusson nearly seventeen years before. Now his youthful buoyancy had been supplanted by a meticulous precision, carrying him from one extreme to the other.

True, he had gained some experience as an actor, but that had caused him to over-rehearse his show until his manner tended to become as mechanical as some of his devices. His opening number, the "Cabalistic Clock," was marvelous indeed. It consisted of a glass dial suspended by ribbons, with a single hand that could be spun about, only to stop on any number that the audience called. But it was too much like Robert's show-window clock to win great applause.

The "Obedient Cards," which rose from the pack at command, had been a favorite with Comte, whose humorous touches had won Robert's admiration, inspiring him to introduce a few fine points of his own. But the audience apparently remembered Comte, for they failed to respond to Robert's version.

It was on the bowl trick that Robert-Houdin banked most strongly. He showed a large shawl, which he termed a magical fishing net, spread it over his arm, and from its folds brought a fish bowl nine inches in diameter, filled with water and goldfish. But as he placed the bowl on a table and took a bow, the audience, though quite amazed, was slow to applaud.

Robert-Houdin's new automata did much to save the show. Two mechanical clowns, Auriol and Debureau, did acrobatic stunts; then one smoked a pipe and accompanied the orchestra on a flute. Blossoms appeared upon an imitation orange tree, followed by ripe fruit. The "Pastry Cook of the Palais Royal" was a figure that went in and out of a miniature shop, bringing refreshments called for by the audience.

However, when the curtain fell, Robert-Houdin was on the

verge of another collapse. He had long felt that life, for a magician, should begin at forty. Having attained that age, he had expected to impress his audience with his composure as well as his ability. Instead, he had raced through the final portion of his program, and he realized now how much he needed the experience that he should have gained in earlier years.

That night, he dreamed he was doing the show over and over, making every possible mistake. Exhausted from such nightmares, he slept most of the next day and finally called off the evening performance, rather than have his fears become realities. Word spread that the new theater had closed to stay, but by the third evening, Robert-Houdin had regained his confidence, and he made his appearance before a small but sympathetic audience.

That evening, the show went better. It improved nightly, and the audiences steadily increased, particularly when Robert-Houdin began receiving commendations from the Parisian press. By studying audience reactions, he was able to improve his methods. Before the fish-bowl production, Robert-Houdin stepped offstage long enough to conceal the fish bowl in a special pocket suspended from his waist beneath the tails of his coat. The bowl had a watertight cover and could be reached with one hand, while a shawl was draped over the other arm. The cover was removed with the shawl, revealing the bowl, but though no one guessed exactly where it came from, the trick failed to create the surprise it should have.

Robert-Houdin decided that the production was too abrupt, coming so soon after he walked onstage. Therefore he devised a prelude called the "Marvelous Equilibrium" in which he balanced a stack of large checkers on the head of an upright cane and set a wineglass on the top. One by one, he knocked away the checkers, leaving the glass undisturbed. He then picked up the shawl and produced the giant bowl. Its contrast with the tiny wineglass made it seem all the more immense, and the delayed production gave the impression that Robert-Houdin might have conjured the bowl from nowhere at any time in his performance.

As he continued his exhibitions, Robert-Houdin injected dozens of other artifices into his routine, while planning new features for his program. Gradually, he was formulating maxims in regard to magic, which have applied ever since. One was that a magician should consider himself to be an actor playing the part of a magician, a qualification that Robert-Houdin, drawing upon his experience as an amateur performer, most aptly fulfilled. Another was that a program should always be arranged to make each trick more surprising than the one that just preceded it.

What Robert-Houdin most needed was a climax to his show that would fill his two-hundred-seat theater to capacity, night after night. He recalled that sixty years before, Pinetti had presented a remarkable experiment, wherein his wife, while blindfolded, had named various articles held up by members of the audience. A version of the trick had been explained by Decremps, one of the magical writers with whose works Robert-Houdin was quite familiar.

Interest in such experiments had waned until Young Master M'Kean, known as the Highland Youth, had appeared in London during the early 1830s, demonstrating his uncanny power of "double sight" before King William IV, by stating whether objects held by members of the audience were composed of gold, silver, brass, or copper. Several years later, a group of three young Highlanders had given a similar exhibition termed "Second Sight," and in 1843, Professor Anderson, Britain's leading magician, had featured "Second Sight" on his program in London, but had limited it to the divination of objects hidden in special boxes.

Robert-Houdin decided that this phase of conjuring could be developed into a tremendous sensation. He had a son named Émile, who was nearly fourteen years old and was already assisting him on the stage. So he trained the boy in a "Second Sight" routine and then concocted a clever story to "explain" the great mystery that he hoped to launch upon a receptive public.

In so doing, Robert-Houdin set a pattern that all great magicians have followed since. He included it among the rules that he later propounded in a book entitled *The Secrets of Conjuring and Magic.* There he declared:

"Although all one says during the course of a performance is—not to mince the matter—a tissue of falsehoods, the performer must sufficiently enter into the part he plays, to himself believe in the reality of his fictitious statements. This belief on his own part will infallibly carry a like conviction to the minds of the spectators."

That rule could very well have been inspired by the way the gullible public "swallowed" the story that Robert-Houdin told about how he "invented" second sight, for it was indeed a grand deception. It ran like this:

One day, Émile was playing in the parlor with his younger brother, Eugène. Between them, they invented a clever game. One blindfolded the other and began touching objects about the room, asking the blindfolded boy to name the objects that he touched. After every hit, they changed places. Their father happened to walk in on this unusual diversion, and noting that Émile had an uncanny ability to guess right, Robert-Houdin decided to test it further.

He took Émile past shop windows and asked him to list the objects that he had noted in a glance. Amazingly, Émile was able to call off as many as forty items, so Robert-Houdin decided that his son must really have the gift of visualizing objects while blindfolded.

Now, on the face of it, this was one of those innocent frauds that all conjurors had a right to use by Robert-Houdin's own rules. Ability to memorize scenes photographically has no connection whatever with clairvoyant power, or extrasensory perception as it is called today. But the story sounded good, and on Thursday, February 12, 1846, Robert-Houdin's program stated:

> In this performance, Monsieur Robert-Houdin's son, who is gifted with a marvelous second sight, after his eyes have been covered with a thick bandage, will designate every object presented to him by the audience.

What was more, Émile did it. Customers began to fill Robert-Houdin's little theater, and they came again, bringing others more skeptical than themselves, to witness the proof of second sight. The act became the rage of Paris, and, as it fulfilled Robert-Houdin's requirement for the perfect mystery, it always formed the termination of the evening's performance.

In his memoirs, Robert-Houdin related numerous instances where spectators insisted on Émile describing unusual objects, or where they brought sealed packages, demanding that the boy name the contents. In such cases, Robert-Houdin conceded later, he had to open the packages secretly to learn what was inside. In short, he intimated that he had to know the nature of an object in order to transmit a mental impression of it, and he kept insisting that memory played a major part.

Actually, it was simply a very clever trick, which Robert-Houdin and Émile must have developed to an expanding degree to keep on bewildering the sophisticated Parisian audiences. But the Scottish boys were good, too, and Phineas T. Barnum, the showman who had bought the writing-and-drawing figure, hired some of the gifted Highlanders and took them to New York, where their "second sight" was a great success.

In his autobiography, Barnum revealed how the act was worked. His explanation ran:

> The mystery, which was merely the result of patient practice, consisted wholly in the manner in which the

question was propounded; in fact, the question invariably carried its own answer; for instance:

"What is this?" meant gold; "Now, what is this?" silver; "Say what is this?" copper. "Tell me what this is," iron; "What is the shape?" long; "Now what shape?" round; "Say what shape," square; "Please say what this is," a watch; "Can you tell what is in this lady's hand?" a purse; "Now, please say what this is," a key; "Come now, what is this?" money; "How much?" a penny; "Now how much?" sixpence; "Say how much?" a quarter of a dollar; "What color is this?" black; "Now what color is this?" red; "Say what color," green and so on, *ad infinitum*. To such perfection was this brought that it was almost impossible to present any object that could not be quite closely described by the blindfolded boy. This is the key to all exhibitions of what is called "second sight."

Barnum was right, though not entirely so. In claiming "Second Sight" as his own invention, Robert-Houdin unquestionably added some unique devices. His repeated presentations before the same audiences demanded this. There were times when Émile's answers involved inscriptions on ancient coins, complicated coats-of-arms, words in foreign languages, or articles that he had never heard of before. If those were relayed too often through the "spoken code" they could overtax it.

So Robert-Houdin needed another method, and he devised one. The electric telegraph had just been introduced in America, and was unknown in France except to a few advanced experimenters, of whom Robert-Houdin was one. In presenting "Second Sight" in his own theater, Robert-Houdin stood at the front of a carpeted stage, while Émile, blindfolded, sat on a stool in the center. As Robert-Houdin held up objects for the boy to name, he could either step on a transmitter beneath the carpet, or have someone operate another transmitter off stage. In either case, Émile received a coded message through slight electric impulses from a floor plate or through a wired stool.

Five years later, Robert-Houdin's program was copied almost in replica by a budding magician named Heller, who utilized the electrical method in performing "Second Sight." That was learned long afterward, thereby explaining Robert-Houdin's secret, which he himself never revealed.

It was not surprising that many of Robert-Houdin's pet effects were pilfered and sold to other magicians. He had no idea how rapid his rise to fame would be, and he entrusted the construction of his earlier paraphernalia to ordinary workmen who were easily bribed to divulge bits of knowledge after they became valuable trade secrets. Moreover, the little theater in the Palais Royal became a mecca for all the magic enthusiasts in Paris, even more of a rendezvous than Papa Rujol's shop. Thus many aspiring young conjurors gained their start through observing and copying the style of this new master of the craft.

The magicians who were already established were also highly appreciative of the way Robert-Houdin was adding new prestige to their art. Among those who came to pay his respects was the old master, Comte, who still gave occasional performances, but had become perhaps more noted for his ventriloquism than his magic.

One night Comte called backstage after the show and invited Robert-Houdin to join some friends in a late supper. As they started down the stairway, Robert-Houdin noted a gold snuffbox in Comte's coat pocket, and knowing that Comte liked jokes, he deftly filched it and left the pocket inside out. When they turned at the landing halfway down, Robert-Houdin heard a call from the office upstairs: "Monsieur Robert-Houdin! Can you come up to the box office at once? I have something urgent to tell you!"

Excusing himself, Robert-Houdin hurried up to the office

only to be met by the dumb stare of a totally puzzled clerk. Just then, the echoes of a gale of laughter drifted up from downstairs. That voice on the landing had been Comte's. He had worked one of his ventriloquial tricks, making Robert-Houdin think the voice came from upstairs; what was more, he timed it so the people below would see his victim turn and dash up in answer to the summons.

Momentarily chagrined, Robert-Houdin started down to meet the laughing group. Comte, acting as the spokesmen, asked in his most serious tone:

"What did that person want up in the office?"

Robert-Houdin affected real surprise: "Can't you guess?"

"Why, no. Who could it have been?"

"The thief, of course. Who else?"

"The thief?" Comte was becoming wary. "What thief?"

"The one who stole your gold snuffbox." Calmly, Robert-Houdin brought the very article from his pocket. "He made a full confession and asked me to return it to you."

That turned the laugh on Comte, whose love of a good joke enabled him to enjoy it as much as anyone. The double jest may have cemented the friendship between the two magicians, for in June, 1846, Robert-Houdin was summoned to a command performance before King Louis Philippe at the Palace of St. Cloud. Considering that Comte had frequently been so honored and that the king had made him a Chevalier of the Legion of Honor, it is quite likely that the king engaged the new master on the recommendation of the old.

A special theater had been prepared for the occasion and a huge van was provided to transport all of Robert-Houdin's equipment from the Palais Royal to the royal palace, so he could perform with his regular stage set. In the center was an elegant table, flanked by two light side stands—round tables called *guéridons*—which he could carry forward or take back, as needed, and therefore use continually. At the sides, there were two consoles, set against the side scenes with projecting supports. Like the *guéridons*, these had short drapes.

Such was the scene unveiled to the elderly Citizen-King Louis Philippe and the members of his court, on the pleasant afternoon when Robert-Houdin, later to be called "King of the Conjurors," presented his usual performance, including the famed demonstration of "Second Sight." But on this occasion, he topped that near-miracle with perhaps the greatest mystery of modern magic that had ever been presented.

Calm and confident, Robert-Houdin stepped forward and borrowed several handkerchiefs from his august audience. He bundled these into a parcel which he laid aside, while he distributed blank cards among the audience, asking persons to write the names of places where they would like the handkerchiefs to go. He then gathered the cards, requesting the king to take three, and from them choose the card most suitable.

Louis Philippe did so. The first card read, "Under the candelabra on the mantel." That, the king decided, would be too easy. The next read, "To the dome of the Invalides." That, the king declared, would be too far away. The third read, "In the chest beneath the third orange tree on the right of the corridor." That suited Louis Philippe. He asked Robert-Houdin to conjure the handkerchiefs to that appointed destination, and the magician declared that he would do so.

It was like the acceptance of a challenge, and Louis Philippe responded in kingly style. He sent attendants to guard the designated orange tree, which was visible through the doors of the temporary theater. Robert-Houdin then picked up the bundled handkerchiefs and a dome-shaped cover of frosted glass. He stepped to the center table, placed the dome over the bundle and clanged the glass with his wand as he announced:

"The handerkerchiefs are gone. Behold!"

Robert-Houdin lifted the glass cover. A white turtledove

31

flew out and lighted upon an elegant chandelier. The hand-kerchiefs had vanished!

Louis Philippe immediately ordered the attendants to open the front of the square-shaped chest in which the orange tree was planted. There they found a small, rusted iron coffer tangled among the tree roots. It was brought to the king, and after earth and mold had been removed, Louis Philippe commented that the ancient chest was locked. Robert-Houdin bowed, lifted the turtledove from its perch and indicated a key attached to the bird's neck. The king used the key to unlock the coffer. Inside he found a parchment bearing the statement:

THIS DAY, THE 6TH OF JUNE, 1786,

this iron box, containing six handkerchiefs, was placed among the roots of an orange tree by myself, Balsamo, Count of Cagliostro, to serve in performing an act of Magic, which will be executed on the same day sixty years hence before Louis Philippe of Orléans and his family.

As the king read the curious document aloud, a murmur swept the audience: "Cagliostro!" Truly that was a name to conjure with, for Joseph Balsamo, self-styled Count of Cagliostro, had been the most controversial figure of his day, a pretended miracle worker who had carried the fanciful claims of sorcerers into the scientific age.

Recently a new novel by Alexandre Dumas had appeared, based on the career of Cagliostro, who had been involved in the intrigues of the French court at the time of the Revolution and might very possibly have planted this antique coffer as the parchment stated. Not only did the parchment bear Cagliostro's seal and signature, there was a packet with it, stamped with the same seal.

Louis Philippe compared the two to his satisfaction, tore open the sealed packet and brought out the very handkerchiefs that

Robert-Houdin had borrowed and vanished. They were returned to their various owners, who identified them and joined the applause for Robert-Houdin, whose modern wizardry outshone the pretended miracles of Cagliostro.

Now to analyze the working of this remarkable mystery:

Robert-Houdin had discarded suspiciously-draped tables placed against the backdrop as in Pinetti's day. Instead, he had introduced artful substitutes—those innocent consoles supported by brackets extending from the side scenes, so close to the footlights that spectators could almost reach up and touch their hanging fringes, though not quite.

The person who *could* reach one of those consoles was Émile, who was concealed behind the side scene. He was able to thrust his arm inside the fringed top, which was hollow, and operate a small trap with his hand. The trap was hinged and its edges were perfectly hidden by the ornamental pattern of the table covering.

Beforehand, Robert-Houdin had prepared a packet of half a dozen handkerchiefs, which were in Émile's custody. After the magician borrowed six similar handkerchiefs from the audience, he came back up on the stage and placed them on the console on the right, directly over the trap. He picked up the glass dome that was purposely lying there, and set it over the packet, stating:

"I shall keep the handkerchiefs safely here until you decide among yourselves just where you would like them to go."

To aid that choice, Robert-Houdin picked up some blank cards and pencils from the console on the right and had an attendant distribute them among the audience. Then he walked across stage to the console on the left, picked up more cards and pencils, and had an attendant distribute them from that side.

This gave Émile time to reach in and release the trap in the console on the right, drawing the borrowed handkerchiefs down from beneath the opaque dome. After checking the packets to make sure they matched, he pushed the duplicates up under the glass bell, closed the trap and locked it.

From then on, Émile was busy indeed. He wrapped the borrowed handkerchiefs in a package, applied some melted wax and affixed it with a genuine Cagliostro seal that Robert-Houdin had brought along for the occasion. He put it in the coffer and added the parchment, which already bore a replica of Cagliostro's signature and had been stamped with the same seal.

Next, Émile locked the coffer and hurried out to the third orange tree, which Robert-Houdin had picked from among a dozen promising hiding places about the garden. The orange tree had worked out nicely for two reasons: first, it had been easy to get into the chest from the back and hollow out enough earth to implant the coffer among the roots; second, the orange tree in question was just out of the audience's sight, yet visible from the doors of the improvised theater.

So while Émile was planting Cagliostro's coffer and fixing the back of the chest firmly in place again, Robert-Houdin was telling the audience to write their suggestions, no matter how impossible they might seem. In the midst of that, he raised the frosted dome from the console, showed the handkerchiefs again, and carried them to his center table, where he set them on the glass dome itself, so they would be in plain sight when the choice of their destination was made.

Here, Robert-Houdin prolonged the act by telling people to take all the time they needed. As soon as he saw Émile arrive backstage, he stepped into the audience and gathered the cards, asking everyone to keep the written side down, rather than let others see their suggestions.

In the left inside pocket of his coat, Robert-Houdin had his own set of cards, bearing just three statements in different handwriting, running in rotation through the entire stack. These referred to the candelabra on the mantel, the dome of the Invalides, and the chest beneath the third orange tree. As he finished gathering the audience's cards in his left hand, he apparently transferred them to his right, as he turned toward the stage.

Actually, while the magician's back was momentarily toward the audience, his hands crossed, and his left hand thrust the original cards into the inside pocket on the right, while his right hand brought the special set from the left inside pocket. Continuing his sweeping turn, Robert-Houdin approached Louis Philippe and invited the king to take a group of three cards from anywhere he pleased. At the same time, the magician spread the cards, but that made no difference; any three, taken together, would be the desired trio, due to the rotation.

The rest was pure psychology. Asked to choose one of the three cards, the king took the one best suited to the occasion, as the magician expected. Back on the stage, Robert-Houdin set the duplicate handkerchiefs on a mechanical "changing trap" in his ornate center table, and covered them with the dome. A press of his wrist, and the handkerchiefs were gone into the table, behind the decorative molding; while a dove, concealed there earlier, popped up beneath the glass, wearing a key to Cagliostro's coffer.

If Louis Philippe had chosen either of the other two cards, Robert-Houdin still could have carried this superb mystery to a successful conclusion. All he needed were two more packets of duplicate handkerchiefs, one wedged in the base of a candelabra on the mantel; the other in the cupola of the Dôme des Invalides above Napoleon's tomb.

In either case, Robert-Houdin would have simply vanished one batch, to find them as stated; then, before returning them to the owners, he would have had a second card selected— and if need be the third!—in order to follow the transformation of handkerchiefs to turtledove with the scheduled discovery of Cagliostro's coffer.

Robert-Houdin knew many ways of vanishing handkerchiefs, including the method used by Philippe, the conjuror, upon which Robert-Houdin had appropriately patterned this magical gem for the benefit of Louis Philippe. In the older version, Philippe had simply switched a batch of borrowed handkerchiefs for duplicates, under cover of his wizard's robe. He had left the duplicates in view on a table, while he stepped offstage to get a blunderbuss.

There, Philippe had handed the borrowed handkerchiefs to his assistant, Domingo, so that while the magician, returning to the stage, was openly loading the duplicates into the gun, Domingo, behind the wings, was secretly loading the originals into a hollow sugar loaf and neatly plugging the hole. When Domingo brought on the sugar loaf, Philippe simply fired the blunderbuss at it, and the trick was done.

This comparison clearly shows that Robert-Houdin's forte was adding refinements to standard magical effects. In the fanciful presentation at the Château of St. Cloud, Robert-Houdin moved from the simple to the complex. He turned a routine trick into a mystery by imposing seemingly impossible conditions; then gave it the aura of real magic by invoking the sorcery of Cagliostro as the only plausible answer to the riddle.

Following his triumph at St. Cloud, Robert-Houdin continued to beguile the patrons of his theater with new and intriguing mysteries. These included the "Crystal Cash Box," in which coins vanished and then reappeared; the "Inexhaustible Bottle," his improved version of a trick in which any drink demanded by the audience was poured from one bottle; and finally, the "Ethereal Suspension," which created an immediate and long-lasting sensation.

Here, as in his presentation of "Second Sight," Robert-Houdin gave a quasi-scientific explanation to a stage mystery. And in this case, too, he introduced one of his sons, this time the younger boy, Eugène.

All Paris was agog over a great medical discovery, an anesthetic called "ether" which the public regarded as nearly miraculous in its results. Trading on that opinion, Robert-Houdin announced that he had experimented with ether and had found it more potent than even medical minds supposed. He had his son stand upon a stool, flanked by two upright rods set in a platform. The boy stretched his arms to rest an elbow on each rod; then Robert-Houdin uncorked a small bottle and had the child inhale from it.

Immediately, the boy went rigid, and the pungent odor of ether, wafting through the audience, certified that the anesthetic was at work. To show the depth of his son's sleep, Robert-Houdin raised the boy's right forearm and tilted his head downward, propping it upon the upraised hand. Carefully, Robert-Houdin removed the stool, and the audience was a bit puzzled to see the boy remain rigid, his arms supporting his full weight.

Then Robert-Houdin took away the pole from beneath the boy's left arm, but his position did not change, even though he was hanging by his right elbow alone. Gently, Robert-Houdin lowered the boy's extended left arm to his side, as though anxious not to disturb his equilibrium. This was surprising enough, but what followed brought gasps from the audience.

Robert-Houdin took hold of the boy's body and lifted it from the vertical to the horizontal. He then stepped away, leaving the boy extended straight out from the pole, poised only on his right elbow, with no other support. Standing by, Robert-Houdin watched with fatherly apprehension until he seemingly detected a slight motion of the boy's head. Immediately, he lowered the child's body, raised his left arm and hurriedly set the extra pole and then the stool in place. At that point, just as if the effects of the ether were wearing off, the boy opened his eyes to stare about, bewildered.

This trick brought letters of outraged protest from squeamish patrons, who insisted that the boy's health was jeopardized by the anesthetics. Actually, ether had nothing to do with the case. The aerial suspension was accomplished by means of a cleverly concealed mechanism, which operated as follows:

Under his costume, the boy wore an iron framework, fitted firmly to his right side by straps fastened around his body. Fixed to the frame was an upright iron bar, extending from knee to armpit, where it joined another bar that ran from armpit to elbow. Below the elbow was an iron pin that fitted into a socket in the upright pole, which was also made of metal.

Once set in place, this supplied all necessary support to hold the boy in a vertical position when the extra pole was removed. The junction of the hidden rods was provided with a semicircular plate and ratchet, which enabled the magician to raise the boy's body to the horizontal and have it retain that posture. A reversal of the process brought the boy back to his original position.

There was no ether in the bottle Eugène sniffed; that was scientific pretense on the part of Robert-Houdin. However the older brother, Émile, was backstage pouring ether on a hot pan, and this was the source of the pungent odor that reached the audience.

During the season of 1847, Robert-Houdin gave another performance before the court. But this time, the king and his entourage came from the royal palace to the Palais Royal. They wanted to see Robert-Houdin perform on his own stage, so they bought out the theater. Truly, Robert-Houdin had become "King of the Conjurors," and his glory was to last longer than that of the royalty he entertained.

In February, 1848, a revolution ended the reign of Louis Philippe, and show business went with it. Robert-Houdin finally locked the door of his little theater, took most of his elegant apparatus to England and joined a company of French dramatists who were at the St. James's Theatre in London. There, Robert-Houdin presented his program three nights a week, and he was twice honored by commands to appear before Queen Victoria and her court.

After his London engagement, Robert-Houdin made a three-month tour of the British Isles, then returned to Paris and reopened his theater for a new and successful season. A few years more, and his performances had become a fixture in the minds of Parisian theatergoers. By 1850, his two sons were old enough for him to hope that one or the other would soon succeed him as the magician of the Palais Royal.

But Émile, then nineteen, decided to become a watchmaker, like both of his grandfathers; while Eugène, just turned thirteen, was eager to enter St. Cyr, the French West Point, and take up an army officer's career. So Robert-Houdin turned over the theater to his brother-in-law, Pierre Chocat, who adopted the stage name of Hamilton, and continued to present the mysteries that Robert-Houdin had made famous.

Theater-owners throughout France had long been begging Robert-Houdin to appear in their cities; now, for the first time, he was able to meet that demand without closing his theater in Paris. For two years, he toured France, then went to Germany where he appeared before many of the lesser princes who were ruling at that time. He arrived in London in the spring of 1853 and again performed for Queen Victoria. After a brief tour through England, he returned to France and retired from the stage, to live in a house that he had built at St. Gervais, near Blois.

Just as he had abandoned watchmaking for conjuring, so did Robert-Houdin lay aside the wand for another type of wizardry, that of the electrical inventor. The secrets of many of his stage devices, such as the "Cabalistic Clock" and the "Crystal Casket," depended on electricity. Now he put that knowledge to more practical uses.

The Priory, as Robert-Houdin called his home, would have been an inspiration to young Tom Edison, who was just then starting out as a newsboy. The visitor's gate had a heavy brass knocker which, when rapped in the usual style, rang a bell in the house, a quarter mile away. There, whoever heard the summons pressed a switch; and the wording of the name plate attached to the distant gate suddenly changed from ROBERT-HOUDIN to ENTREZ-VOUS, meaning "Walk in."

When someone did, the gate closed automatically, actuating another bell. An immediate ring indicated that the caller was a friend, who had been watching for the words "Walk in." A delayed ring indicated a stranger, who had stared in surprise. A short ring meant one visitor; by counting intermittent rings, Robert-Houdin could tell when there were more, and how many. Other of Robert-Houdin's inventions included an automatic feeder for his horse and an electric thermostat that regulated the temperature of his hothouse or rang bells in case of fire or burglary. All his clocks were synchronized by an electrical timer, putting Robert-Houdin's home a century ahead of its day.

While Robert-Houdin was working on these devices in 1854, Colonel de Neveu, of the French office in Algiers, invited him there to impress the Arab chieftains with his magic. Fanatical wonder-workers called Marabouts were inciting Algerian tribes to revolt, and the colonel wanted to show them that a French magician could more than match their marvels.

Due to other commitments, it was not until September, 1856, that Robert-Houdin embarked on his singular mission. Upon reaching Algiers with his equipment, he learned that revolts in the Kabylia district had caused the assemblage to be postponed for a month, so he arranged to appear twice a week at the city theater, sandwiching his dates between those of an opera company.

When the Arab chieftains arrived for the annual fete, Robert-Houdin was back in form after his three-year layoff. Few of the visiting sheiks and their roving followers had ever been in a theater before, let alone seen a European-style magical performance. For that reason, the show itself was different from any Robert-Houdin had ever given. He had selected from his long repertoire only those tricks that both he and Colonel de Neveu felt would appeal to the superstitious minds of this unsophisticated audience.

Early in the program, Robert-Houdin began producing articles from a hat, among them cannon balls, which he let thump on the stage, an old trick to Europeans, but one that brought excited cries from the Arabs. Tricks with money, candy, and the production of steaming coffee—all sure-fire with juvenile groups—were received with almost childish glee.

But the show was building to its serious side. This came with the "Light and Heavy Chest," which Robert-Houdin had frequently presented at the Palais Royal. The chest was a small but solidly constructed box, which he invited people to lift from a runway extending into the audience, telling them he could make it become light or heavy at will.

Parisians had roared with laughter, watching grown men struggle unsuccessfully to lift the mysterious box, only to have a child pick it up with ease. Here in Algiers, however, Robert-Houdin played it straight. Though he had amused this audience, he knew that he had also won their awe, so rather than announce his next experiment as a "Light and Heavy Chest," he boldly declared that he would turn the strongest man present into a helpless weakling at command.

The audience buzzed excitedly when the interpreter translated that challenge. When Robert-Houdin added that he was waiting for a volunteer, a dozen robed men sprang to their feet. The magician accepted the first who reached the stage, showed him the miniature chest, placed it on the runway and said:

"Lift up this box."

Between what French he knew, and the magician's gesture, the Arab understood. He lifted the box and replaced it; then stood with folded arms, as if asking: "What next?"

41

Through an interpreter, Robert-Houdin announced that he was already depriving the volunteer of his strength. He made mesmeric passes to stress the fact, but when he pointed to the box, and said, "Now lift!" the Arab's smile became disdainful. He gripped the handle, intending to whip the chest high in the air, then straightened up with every muscle strained.

Despite his great strength, he could not budge the chest!

Again, he bent over it, gripping and tugging the handle with both hands, but to no avail, though it seemed that if he could not lift the chest, he might manage to rip it apart. However, Robert-Houdin was prepared for that, too. He waved his hand, and the strong man's efforts were turned to frantic contortions. As he writhed about, still clutching the box handle, Robert-Houdin gave another gesture, and the Arab, suddenly letting go of the handle, reeled back, jumped to the aisle and raced out of the theater, covering his head with his robe and screaming.

The secret of the act was this: When Robert-Houdin had first wired his stage, he had hooked an electromagnet under the cloth that covered the runway, fitting it into a cut-out space. The conducting wires ran to a switch offstage, and the chest had an iron plate in the bottom. When an assistant pressed the switch, the magnet took hold and it was impossible to lift the box until the current was cut off.

Anticipating trouble on this occasion, Robert-Houdin had also wired the handles of the box, so that his assistant could jolt the volunteer with an electric shock. That accounted for the Arab's contortions and finally his flight. Robert-Houdin had simply given the signals for "On" and "Off."

Having demonstrated his own incredible powers, Robert-Houdin now proceeded to match those of the Marabouts. Colonel de Neveu had told him that the Algerian wizards claimed no bullets could harm them, so it would be wise for a French magician to prove that he had the same immunity.

Robert-Houdin called for another volunteer, allowed him to load a pistol and aim straight for the magician's heart.

With a gleaming smile, the Arab exclaimed happily, "I will kill you!" as he fired point-blank. At that instant, Robert-Houdin interposed an apple on the point of a knife. The bullet, instead of finding his body, lodged in the heart of the apple, which was cut open to reveal it!

It was the tragic trick that had killed Torrini's son, Giovanni. Nearly thirty years ago, young Jean Robert had heard the grim story from Torrini himself, and ever since, he had assiduously avoided the gun trick. But now, when his career was all but closed, he had dared fate. If ever a time called for a magician to perform the bullet trick, this was it.

As the audience sat overawed, Robert-Houdin called for another volunteer, without specifying a purpose. While others hesitated, a solemn-faced Moor came up on the stage and Robert-Houdin invited him to stand upon a table that had an open space beneath. A huge cone was lowered over the unsuspecting volunteer at the magician's command. During a tense wait, the audience became more excited than ever, until Robert-Houdin ordered the cone to be lifted.

It was raised and the Moor was gone!

That broke up the show. The spectators raced from the theater, each fearful that he would be the next victim of Robert-Houdin's sorcery. Outside, they encountered the very man who had just vanished, but before they could ask him what had happened, he turned and ran away.

Robert-Houdin had often worked that trick, using his son Émile, who slid through a trap into the table, which was just deep enough to hide him when the cone was lifted. On this occasion, Robert-Houdin had used a Moorish confederate whom he had rehearsed in the cone trick, and who was prompt to step on the stage at the proper moment.

The Moor had been chosen for the part because he had a twin brother, who was also a confederate. He was the one

43

who was waiting outside to meet the excited spectators, and who had ran away before they had time to question him.

Since the theater was only large enough to hold half of the visiting tribesmen, Robert-Houdin repeated his performance the next night, with the same sensational success. Soon afterward, he returned to France, where he filled a short farewell engagement in Marseilles, and then retired to St. Gervais.

For fifteen years, Robert-Houdin continued his experiments and wrote his memoirs, which he followed with a textbook on magic that still stands as one of the finest in the field. He was at work on a further volume when he suffered a loss as great as Torrini's. Early in the Franco-Prussian War, his son Eugène, a captain in a Zouave regiment, was mortally wounded at the Battle of Wörth on August 6, 1870, and died four days later.

In October, the Germans occupied Orléans and a French army corps was hastily formed at Blois to prevent a march on Tours. As the tide of war surged back and forth, Robert-Houdin constructed a secret cave near the Priory, where he stored valuables belonging to his friends, until peace was declared in February, 1871. The invaders never did reach Blois, but the rigor of that winter took its toll.

Sorrowed by his son's death, his strength overtaxed from his wartime effort, Robert-Houdin succumbed to an attack of pneumonia and died on June 13, 1871, at the age of sixty-five. But they still remember him in Blois, where, as a youth, he fancied there might some day be a street called the Rue Jean Eugène Robert, in honor of a great watchmaker-to-be.

There is no such street in Blois, but if you happen to be in that picturesque old town, not far from the bookseller's shop where young Jean Robert picked up the wrong volumes by mistake you may see a sign that should strike a familiar note. The name upon it reads:

RUE ROBERT-HOUDIN

44

Chapter 2

Professor Anderson

(1814–1874)

"They call me the Wizard of the North, but they are wrong. That title rightfully belongs to you."

Those words were attributed to Sir Walter Scott, the great historical novelist, after he witnessed a performance given by John Henry Anderson, a budding young magician from Aberdeen. The time was late in 1830, or early in 1831, and the place was Scott's beautiful mansion Abbotsford, by the river Tweed in Scotland.

Some skeptics have cast doubt on this story, yet it is quite possible that Scott, then in the last few years of his life, may have invited Anderson to perform at Abbotsford. Scott had just finished writing his famous *Letters on Demonology and Witchcraft*, which showed his intense interest in all forms of mystery. Then, too, we have Anderson's own word for it, though Anderson, like every magician before or since, had a way of solemnly telling people things he didn't really expect them to believe.

In any case the fact remains that Anderson did become one of the greatest wizards of his time and perhaps of all time, for he turned magic into a grand spectacle that countless thousands thronged to see.

John Henry Anderson was born on a little farm near Aberdeen, where both his parents died before he was ten years old. He was placed with a traveling theatrical company, in which he served as call boy, summoning the actors when they were due on stage, and running errands. Soon he was playing small parts. During his teens, he became a full-fledged actor, appearing as Romeo in *Romeo and Juliet*.

The youth's travels took him through England, where, between shows, he visited fairs and witnessed magical performances by such noted conjurors as Signor Blitz and Ingleby Lunar. Magic completely intrigued young Anderson, for he was quick to recognize the transition that the art was undergoing during the late 1820s.

At the fairs, magicians worked in booths. When performing indoors, they copied that arrangement by setting the stage like a curtained alcove, with a heavily draped table at the front. A pack of cards, a pistol, a bottle, a funnel, a few boxes, some eggs and a pair of lighted candles were their chief apparatus, with some elaborate automatic figures as feature attractions.

From behind the table, the magician went through his routine, trick by trick. A written slip of paper was burned in a candle flame, then found restored inside the candle itself. A chosen card jumped from the pack at command. An egg was balanced on a cane and made to dance along it. Articles placed on the table and covered with a cone underwent immediate transformations, such as an orange turning into a block of wood spotted to resemble a die.

The more Anderson witnessed these marvels, the simpler they seemed. Substitution of a written paper for a blank and a switch of one candle for another accounted for the burning and restoration. The jumping card and the dancing egg were both actuated by an unseen thread. An assistant hidden in the table drew down objects through a secret trap and pushed up others to replace them.

A comedy number in which the magician pumped water from a spectator's elbow was accomplished with the aid of a double funnel, a smaller inside a larger. The water stayed in the hidden space between them until the magician removed his finger from an air hole beneath the handle of the funnel; then the liquid poured down into a waiting glass.

The better conjurors, like Blitz and Ingleby, were less brazen in their technique. Their exchanges were more cleverly done, their presentations more effective. Blitz, for example, interspersed his magic with ventriloquism, plate-spinning and an act with trained birds, while his automata were almost a show in themselves. He featured a magic portfolio which he folded flat, then opened, producing such substantial items as pictures, bonnets, small handbags and even square cages containing live birds.

Audiences were amazed by such productions, but to young Anderson's now practiced eye, it was obvious that all the items were either flat or collapsible, so that they could be stowed in the supposedly empty portfolio beforehand.

Ingleby Lunar presented a program similar to Blitz's, including performing birds as well as automata. His magic was rather commonplace, but his advertising was extravagant, promising fantastic marvels that even a real miracle man could hardly have accomplished. He managed to brush off those exaggerations during his performances, satisfying his audiences with lesser mysteries that made them forget his grandiose claims.

Anderson dreamed of turning these fantasies into reality. He pictured a temple of magic that could be truthfully advertised as such, with a stage setting so elaborate that the audience would be overwhelmed at first sight. In it, he would perform magic on a grand scale, with all the dramatic quality of a play.

Anderson had one great advantage over his predecessors and competitors: he was an actor first and a magician afterward, which enabled him to gauge his audiences accurately. He was also enraptured by the thrill of conjuring and was able to couple sincerity with make-believe. Acquiring apparatus was not difficult, for magic was on the upsurge, with would-be conjurors cropping up everywhere. Through his contacts with showmen, young Anderson soon assembled a repertoire of workable tricks to which he applied his own individual style of presentation.

In the fall of 1831, Anderson hired a hall in Aberdeen and put on a dramatic show in which he introduced his magic as a special feature. His success was such that he soon expanded his magic into a full evening performance and embarked upon the career that was to make him an acknowledged master of the conjuring craft.

Anderson hired a man named Scott (no relation to Sir Walter) to serve as his instructor in magic. Scott was an old-time magician who lived in Aberdeen and gave such fanciful accounts of his life that everyone called him "Baron Munchausen" in honor of the fictional character who was classed as the world's greatest liar. To back his tall tales, the Baron boasted of the times he had performed the "Bullet Catching Trick," and he had a huge scar on one side of his face as a souvenir of an occasion when the trick had gone wrong. That no one doubted, for magicians had already begun to abandon the bullet catch as too dangerous to be risked.

The trick was the invention of Philip Astley, a famous riding master and circus owner, who had died at the age of seventy-two in 1814, the year in which John Henry Anderson was born. Astley had doubled as an acrobat and had performed as a conjuror as well. In 1785 he had published a book on *Natural Magic* which, except for the final trick, was simply a translation of a volume written by the Frenchman Decremps a few years before.

The last trick was the "Bullet Catch," and Astley told how he devised it to prevent two army officers from being killed in a foolhardy duel. Their pistols were loaded, they fired point-blank at each other, but without result, because Astley, who had loaded the guns, secretly extracted the bullets

48

without their knowledge. From that, Astley developed the trick so that a gun loaded with a marked bullet could be fired at a magician, who would calmly catch the bullet on the point of a knife.

The method was simple but deceptive. The pistols of that period were muzzle-loaders. First, powder was poured in, then a bullet was dropped in and rammed tight with a metal rod. Finally, a wad of paper was rammed home to hold the load in place, so the gun could be leveled and fired.

Astley's addition was a small metal tube, about two inches long, open at one end, closed at the other. The magician held this concealed in the fingers of one hand. After pouring the powder down into the muzzle, he took the pistol with his finger tips and secretly let the little tube drop into the gun. The bullet was dropped in next and slid into the open end of the tube.

The magician proceeded to ram down the bullet, and in so doing, jammed the ramrod into the tube, bringing it out, bullet and all. Wadding was then inserted in the muzzle and rammed down with the other end of the ramrod. The little tube simply passed as the end of the ramrod, which it matched in diameter and color.

When the magician gave the gun to a spectator and walked away, he took the ramrod with him. By detaching the tube from the ramrod, he secretly obtained the marked bullet, which the spectators supposed was still in the gun. He then impaled the bullet on one point of a knife that had two blades, one extending upward, the other downward.

In exhibiting the knife, the magician kept the point with the bullet downward, so that it was concealed within his hand. Next he invited the spectator to fire. Timed to the report of the gun, the magician thrust his hand upward, reversing the knife with a dexterous flip, and bringing the lower blade in sight with the bullet on its tip.

The trick was sensational and, from the magician's standpoint, it seemed sure and safe, for he never gave the word to fire until he had the bullet ready. But while he was engaged in that operation, he had no control over the spectator who served as marksman. As an added test, the spectator was apt to drop a missile of his own into the gun.

In Scott's case, it had been a button, hence the scar. Other magicians fared worse. One named Buck, performing in Ireland, met up with a marksman who broke off the stem of his clay pipe and added it to the charge, injuring the magician seriously. Others were killed performing the bullet trick. Scott's sincere advice to Anderson was, "Don't do it."

But Anderson not only performed the trick, he improved it. He decided that the problem lay with the marksman, not the magician. If he kept his eye on the man with the gun, his own part would be easy. He developed a composition bullet, as hard as soft lead, but formed of an amalgam that would blow apart like the paper wad that was rammed into the gun to hold the charge in place.

Once a lead bullet was marked, Anderson switched it for the imitation, which bore another mark. This was given to the man who was to fire the gun, but not having seen the original bullet, he did not know the difference. What was more, he never suspected the switch, because he never saw Anderson touch the bullet.

The magician received the marked bullet on a silver platter with a small well in the center. A hidden slide, which he drew back from beneath, carried the real bullet from sight and left the dummy in its place. The silver platter went off stage and the real bullet was slipped to Anderson later, after he had watched the entire loading process. Still, the trick could go wrong, as Anderson was to learn.

While performing in Aberdeen and the surrounding country, Anderson was invited to appear before Lord Panmure at Brechin Castle, on February 23, 1837. That performance won him such acclaim that he adopted the title of "Professor" and went on an extensive tour, winding up in Glasgow. There he built a Temple of Magic with seats for two thousand spectators, and in 1839 was heralded as "the Great Caledonian Magician."

The very size of the auditorium demanded a huge stage setting. Anderson's equipment now included ornate tables, pedestals and boxes, with tiers of glass and silver apparatus which he claimed were fashioned from a special alloy with magical propensities. The scene was illuminated by hundreds of candles in great chandeliers, a far cry from the dim booths and dusky alcoves in which some outmoded conjurors still performed.

In 1840, Anderson arrived in London, where he billed himself as the "Great Wizard of the North." His performances proved so popular that he stayed for more than six months and received a royal command to appear before Queen Victoria. For the next four years, the Wizard played annual engagements at the Adelphi Theatre in London, advertising himself on a grand scale.

Among his attractions was "The Animated Oranges, the Dissolving Rabbit and the Flying Guinea Pig," which miraculously changed places between two boxes with sliding drawers and a large silver vase. These, of course, had double compartments that were quite unsuspected by the unsophisticated audiences of that period, and in fact are still occasionally used by magicians today.

The "Dissolving Dice" were described in Anderson's program as large "blocks of ebony marked with spots of ivory." These passed from a silver case through the crowns of hats borrowed from the audience. Two hats were placed brim to brim, one upon the other, and a solid five-inch die was set on top. Anderson lifted the upper hat, tilted it, and let the die drop into the lower hat. He took the die out, replaced the upper hat on the lower and again put the die on top.

Then he accomplished the same result by magic. He covered

the die with the silver case, which he immediately lifted to show that the wooden block had gone. Amazingly, it was found in the lower hat. The trick was repeated with another die and two more borrowed hats, much to the mystification of the audience.

Each die was provided with a five-sided "shell" fitting over it snugly, like a cover. The shell was spotted exactly like the die and both were shown as one. But after they were dropped into the lower hat, only the shell was brought out. It was placed upon the upper hat, where it passed as the solid die. It was then covered with the silver case, which also fitted snugly.

The silver case, when lifted, could be shown apparently empty, because its interior was matched by that of the hollow shell. The discovery of the solid die in the lower hat completed the magical penetration. Improved forms of this trick are still presented by magicians today.

Under the head of "Phoenixsistography" the Wizard introduced an "extraordinary delusion" which was simply the burnt paper restored in the candle, but Anderson inspired awe by borrowing a bank note up to the denomination of a thousand pounds and apparently burning it before the horrified owner's eyes. This trick was a tribute to the Professor's skill at sleight of hand, which he never neglected despite his emphasis on apparatus.

In "Ambidextrous Prestidigitation" a borrowed ring traveled from one case to another. It was then tied to a ribbon around the neck of a canary, which vanished from a larger box. An orange was cut open and from its center flew the canary, still carrying the borrowed ring. This "most beautiful, soul-delighting delusion," as it was termed, would still be a good number in a modern magician's act.

Anderson handled it quite ambidextrously. He neatly switched the borrowed ring for another and slipped the original ring to an assistant who carried it offstage. Anderson then placed the substitute ring in a small double-bottomed case from which it "vanished" and "reappeared" in a similar case in the form of a duplicate ring.

Two ladies in the audience held the cases during this magical transposition, and the byplay gave the assistant time to tie the original ring to a canary, which he placed in an imitation orange studded with air holes. The orange was strung on a ribbon that ran across the stage, so it was hanging there when Anderson came up from the audience flourishing the duplicate ring.

The assistant brought on a second canary and the larger box which he placed on a table. Anderson attached the duplicate ring to the bird's neck and put it in the box, where it went through a trap into the table. The box was then shown empty, and when the twin canary flew from the center of the orange, bringing the borrowed ring that was returned directly to its owner, the audience was completely baffled.

Anderson's "Divination or Second Sight" consisted of naming and describing articles placed within a mother-of-pearl case. In his announcement, he declared that "the Wizard is the only living being of the present age who is endowed with this miraculous gift." He neglected to add that he alone owned a mother-of-pearl case with a trick gadget enabling him to open a secret panel and get a look inside without anyone noticing it.

During his repeated London engagements, which ran to a total of seventy-two weeks, Anderson introduced dozens of other novel mysteries on the Adelphi's stage. His "Magic Caldron" was a flashback to his days as a Shakespearian actor, for it resembled the Witches' Scene in *Macbeth*, and Anderson presented it in equally dramatic style.

The Wizard showed a large metal caldron, supported by chains from a tripod, and tilted it so the audience could see that it was empty. Water was poured into the caldron as it hung suspended above a fire, and dummy pigeons were tossed into the witch's brew. In less time than it took to say

"Double, double, toil and trouble," live pigeons came flying from the bubbling pot.

The caldron was ingeniously fitted with a double bottom with compartments containing the pigeons. The water flowed down through a central tube to a deeper section beneath. A hidden catch, when secretly operated, opened the compartments and released the birds. This trick has survived in a modern version in which ducks appear from a tub of water.

The "Miraculous Umbrella" was another of Anderson's novelties during those lush seasons at the Adelphi. An umbrella was shown open, then closed, and placed in a cylindrical case. Anderson then borrowed some handkerchiefs from the audience, tore them into strips which he placed in a gun, and fired the strips at the umbrella. When the umbella was taken from the case, its cover was gone; instead, the torn strips were dangling from the tips of the umbrella's ribs. Anderson detached the strips, placed them in a box and restored them into the borrowed handkerchiefs.

Two umbrellas and a double case accounted for this mystery, while the handkerchiefs were switched early in the trick and later put in one of Anderson's special change boxes. The umbrella trick is still performed today, in a much fancier form, but it is doubtful that it baffles audiences as completely as when Anderson first introduced it.

One of Anderson's pet systems of reclaiming vanished handkerchiefs was to crack open a large bottle and find them inside. To prove that the bottle was normal at the outset, he poured liquid from it. During one of his runs in London, he added a new mystery by pouring out five different drinks before he broke the bottle: wine, water, port, sherry and champagne.

That brought a glowing review in a London newspaper, and *Punch*, the British humor magazine, made a political cartoon of it in April, 1843. For a while, Anderson called the trick "Water versus Wine," but it later became known as the

"Inexhaustible Bottle," and dozens of different liquors were apparently poured from it. As such, the trick remained popular for years and has been performed by many famous magicians up until the present.

The bottle was divided into five different sections, each with its own separate spout, feeding into the bottle neck. Each section had an individual air hole and by pressing his fingers over these, the Wizard prevented the liquids from flowing. Once he lifted a finger, that compartment was free to flow, so whatever drink was called for could be poured.

If handkerchiefs were to be found in the bottle later, the lower portion was faked and the liquids confined to compartments in the top part only. Sometimes doves were produced when the bottle was broken, but as audiences kept calling for more and more drinks, that became the chief feature, and the breaking of the bottle was generally eliminated.

Additional drinks were furnished by having essences and coloring matter in the bottoms of various glasses, and pouring neutral spirits or diluted alcohol from one of the bottle's compartments. The glasses were very small and narrow, so dozens of such synthetic drinks could be poured and served to the audience.

Several other magicians performed the bottle trick prior to Anderson, but he did the most to popularize it. Yet, curiously, Robert-Houdin claimed that he invented the "Inexhaustible Bottle" a few years after Anderson first presented it. Very probably, Robert-Houdin constructed the finest bottle of its type, for he was an excellent mechanic.

Professor Louis Hoffmann, in *Modern Magic*, describes an improved bottle that was truly inexhaustible. It consisted of the usual bottle encased in an outer shell. When running short on drinks, the magician would set it on a draped table attached to the side scene, planting it on two guide pins. This enabled an assistant to reach in beneath the table, draw the inner bottle down through a trap, and push up a filled inner lining in its place. The magician could then go on pouring drinks and even come back for a further supply if needed. Robert-Houdin used such side stands in his stage set; but Hoffmann does not state who invented the refillable bottle.

At the finish of his fourth season at the Adelphi, Anderson was featuring the "Bullet Catch" as a special attraction, inviting people to bring their own guns. This made no difference as long as Anderson supplied the bullets, but it did bring serious challengers up on the stage. That was how Anderson came to be confronted with a grim situation in which the trick went wrong.

Anderson was showing the genuine bullet to a committee, composed of persons invited from the audience and someone had just scratched it for identification, when the man who was to serve as marksman stepped up and declared, "Fine. I'll take the bullet and load it right now." It was done before Anderson had a chance to switch the real bullet for the dummy, and from the triumphant look on the marksman's face, it was plain that he had guessed enough of the trick to know that he had the Wizard of the North at his mercy.

In showing his hand that soon, however, the marksman hadn't reckoned with the Wizard's mettle. Anderson, tall and dynamic, was always at his dramatic best when he performed the gun trick. He watched the marksman load the gun, then stepped back with dignified calm, tapped his chest and coolly ordered: "Aim here—and fire when you wish!"

Anderson wore a half smile as his eye met the marksman's. The audience became tense, as always, when Anderson played up the pretended duel. This time, however, it was real, though only the Wizard and his challenger knew it. Anderson watched the rising gun muzzle and the slow tightening of the marksman's trigger finger. Seconds passed, and the audience began wondering why the marksman hesitated.

Then the challenger's nerve broke. Suddenly, his hand went shaky and he let the gun muzzle drop. He had gone the limit, expecting the Wizard to call quits. Instead, Anderson had thrown the burden on his opponent.

Before the marksman could reason himself into renewing the challenge, realizing that Anderson was the one who would have to give in, the Great Wizard was striding forward, cool as ever. There was sympathy in his smile as he said in a consoling tone: "Don't feel too badly. Others have lost their nerve, thinking they might kill me. You wouldn't want to kill me either, would you now?"

Almost gently, Anderson plucked the gun from the challenger's grasp and showed him back to his seat in the audience. By the time the man was settled there, he would gladly have killed Anderson, but now his chance was gone. The Wizard was back on the steps to the stage, dangling the gun carelessly, looking hopefully at the sea of faces and asking with that same smile:

"Is anyone else willing to volunteer?"

One man was, so Anderson unloaded the gun to let the new marksman load it himself. That gave Anderson his chance to make the bullet switch. He took his stance, gave the word "Fire!" and caught the marked bullet in his accustomed style, to receive the thunderous applause of an audience that was more than usually impressed, though they did not fully realize why.

From London, Anderson went to Glasgow and invested his accumulated fortune in a theater that was designed for great dramatic shows as well as magical spectacles. The new playhouse stood on Glasgow Green beside the river Clyde, and its first season was nicely under way when a fire broke out during a rehearsal. Anderson was dragged away while trying to save some of his precious conjuring equipment and he watched the holocaust from Glasgow Bridge, grimly lamenting that he was unable to charge admission for the greatest show that he had ever staged.

Half the population of Glasgow watched the new City

57

Theatre burn to the ground; at a penny a head, Anderson would have made a fortune. Instead, he lost one, that night of November 18, 1845, for the master showman was left with only five pounds.

But his name was still known. People still craved to see the Great Wizard at the very time when he was ready to abandon his title in favor of the legitimate stage. Nor did he need the massive equipment of magical metal that had melted down with his amalgam bullets. His smaller tricks, combined with his dramatic ability, brought him both audiences and profits during a whirlwind tour of Scotland and northern England. Next, he was off on a tour of Europe, gathering equipment along the way, until he had enough to hire the Alexandrisky Theater in St. Petersburg and put on a full season there.

So great was Anderson's success that he was summoned to give a command performance before the Czar of Russia at the Winter Palace. He continued his tour to Vienna, Berlin and other European cities, arriving back in London late in 1846. There he appeared at Covent Garden, the largest theater in the British capital. Again, the fame of Anderson's wizardry gained him a command performance before Queen Victoria and the Royal Family, this time at Balmoral Castle.

On that occasion, Anderson produced a special brand of Scotch whisky from the "Inexhaustible Bottle." He also introduced an elaborated version of his "Magic Scrap Book," based on the portfolio of Signor Blitz. Plates, glasses, goldfish globes came from the pages of the magic book along with the usual handbags and bird cages. When the Wizard produced a live goose and topped that by bringing his young son in Highland costume from the mysterious volume, it was, indeed, a royal entertainment.

There were two ways of managing these bulkier productions from the flat interior of the enlarged portfolio. One was to set it on a draped table that contained the loads and draw them up through. The other was to tilt a front portion of the album forward from the easel on which it rested, momentarily filling the gap between the easel and the stage. The boy was thrust up from a trap at that instant, secretly taking his place behind the sketchbook and later moving inside it.

From the start of his career, Anderson was plagued by imitators who copied not only his magical effects but his style, manner and advertising methods. Most flagrant of Anderson's major imitators was Bernado or "Barney" Eagle, an illiterate performer who copied Anderson's high-sounding playbills even though he could not read them. Eagle called himself the "Wizard of the South," but some of Anderson's lesser imitators were outright impostors. Some billed themselves as the "Wizard of the North" and at least one small-fry performer toured the British Isles posing as Professor Anderson himself.

It was not overly difficult to imitate Anderson's tricks because he originated very few of them. He had the true showman's philosophy, that of giving the public what it wanted, rather than what he wanted to give it. Anderson saw no reason why a magician should invent his own tricks any more than an actor should write his own plays, or a singer compose his own songs.

But Anderson's manner and his presentation were his own and they were hard to copy. As a youthful magician, he was handsome and debonair; as he matured, he added dignity to his fuller face with a mustache; and at later periods, he wore a beard as well. Anderson also kept ahead of his imitators by building and buying bigger and better apparatus, so that his show always outmatched others with its splendor.

In his advertising, Anderson eclipsed all rivals. Huge posters depicted him as the Napoleon of Necromancy returning triumphantly from Elba. Following the Crimean War, his posters announced that his audiences would be more astonished than the Russians at Sebastopol. His clever handbills and announcements teemed with caricatures and anticipated modern comic art, even to the statements in voice balloons.

He was always bidding towns "farewell," giving the public its last chance to see the Great Wizard. Such posters frequently depicted cupids, elves and other sprites brooding over the Wizard's departure. These were the prototypes of the red devils that were to adorn the showbills of magicians in a later era.

Anderson's advertising also contained poetical effusions, such as the gem that was printed in the seaside town of Brighton while he was playing there. It ran:

> We've the Great Northern Wizard,
> Old Nick in a vizard,
> A fiend, though a very polite one.
> He'll take watch, purse and locket,
> Your eye from its socket,
> Or your head from your shoulders,
> In Brighton!

One of Anderson's great stunts was the offering of prizes for the best riddles submitted by the audience. People turned in their jokes at the door; and during the show, a press busily printed pamphlets containing all the riddles with the names of the persons who submitted them. On the way out, the booklets were sold at a shilling apiece and practically everybody bought one or more.

In 1848, Anderson encountered real competition in London when Carl Herrmann appeared there. Herrmann's style was more mysterious than Anderson's and he depended on his skill at sleight of hand rather than on equipment, though he presented such sensational novelties as the production of gold-fish bowls, the aerial suspension, and a two-person mind-reading act which he styled "Second Sight."

Those effects had been originated by Robert-Houdin, who arrived in London in July to play alternating dates with a French dramatic company. Herrmann had also presented the

"Inexhaustible Bottle" and the "Magic Portfolio," both of which were in Robert-Houdin's programs. Possibly that was why Robert-Houdin claimed to have invented them, for originality was almost a mania where he was concerned, though he included improvements and adaptations under that general head.

Anderson had been appearing at the Strand Theatre since May, and when he shortly concluded his engagement, Robert-Houdin whimsically took credit for driving him back to the provinces where he belonged. That could hardly be taken seriously, for Anderson had already played two months and it was now the summer season. Besides, Robert-Houdin was giving his show in French, which lacked appeal to the mass audiences that Anderson sought.

Anderson was back at the Strand Theatre by Christmas and doing big business. He featured the "Magic Scrap Book" and included the "Aerial Suspension" and the "Bowl Production" in his program, along with the new "Second Sight." Evidently Anderson regarded that as turnabout, fair play, considering that both Herrmann and Robert-Houdin had borrowed his "Bottle Trick" and had taken the title of his older version of "Second Sight."

Anderson's travels brought him into many amusing situations. Once Phineas T. Barnum was exhibiting the celebrated dwarf Tom Thumb at a hall where Anderson's show was to open a few nights later. Anderson knew Barnum, so he dropped around and invited him to a late supper. As they were talking, Anderson began introducing Barnum to strangers as the Wizard of the North.

Soon, people were asking Barnum to do a few tricks and Anderson was passing the word to newcomers that the "Wizard" was about to perform. Barnum begged off, claiming that he was too tired, and Anderson thought he had him on the spot.

Then, Barnum suddenly declared: "Well, gentlemen, as I

61

perform here for the first time on Monday evening, I would like to be liberal and I should be very happy to give orders of admission to those of you who will attend my exhibition."

With that, Barnum began writing passes and signing them with Anderson's name, much to the consternation of the real Wizard, who admitted his identity and called a prompt halt. All present agreed that Barnum had gotten the better of Anderson's little joke.

In Anderson's native Scotland, his fame spread like wildfire—sometimes too wildly. At one inn where Anderson wanted to stop, the landlord flatly refused him, saying he had heard that the Wizard was in league with the devil. When Anderson argued the point, the landlord called on friends who arrived with loaded guns.

The landlord then added that he knew of Anderson's skill at catching bullets, but that this time it would be to no avail. The landlord's friends had loaded their guns with silver sixpences, because according to an old tradition, no witch—nor wizard either—could defy a silver bullet.

Anderson finally convinced the group that his wizardry was of an innocent sort, with no satanic connections. He was then given a room, but the landlord was advised by friends to keep a close watch on his money, or the Wizard might conjure it away. To prevent that, the landlord secretly stuffed all his cash in his bed pillow and kept an eye on Anderson instead. To his horror, when he later checked the pillow, he found that the money had completely vanished.

In no time, Anderson was hauled off to a magistrate, who took a more sensible view of the situation and demanded an intelligent investigation. It turned out that a maid, making up extra beds, had run out of available pillows and had borrowed the landlord's, intending to tell him later. So the innkeeper recovered his hoard and the Wizard was exonerated.

In 1850, Anderson took his show to America and toured the entire United States during that year and the next. Anderson drew bigger audiences than any other performer of the time except the famous Swedish concert singer, Jenny Lind. In New York, Miss Lind attended one of the Great Wizard's performances with her manager, Anderson's old friend, P. T. Barnum. Like other celebrities present, they hopefully contributed riddles to one of Anderson's famous contests.

America was then agog over so-called "spirit rappings," and Anderson delved into the ways of fake mediums sufficiently to bring back an array of spook tricks that he presented in England as "Half-an-hour with the Spirits."

In the summer of 1853, Anderson started from Aberdeen on a farewell tour, for he had made a fortune and was able to retire. But he was only forty, and new successes, including another command performance at Balmoral, spurred him to further fame. In London, after three months of sell-out performances, he closed his magic show on Christmas Eve, 1855, and announced that from then on, he would appear as a dramatic actor.

Anderson hired Covent Garden and played the hero in the popular drama *Rob Roy*, a part with which he was thoroughly familiar. But Anderson the actor was less successful than Anderson the magician. After two months, during which the new venture just about broke even, Anderson advertised a grand carnival that was to last for two days and two nights.

The gala festival included an opera, a drama in which Anderson played the lead, a burlesque, a pantomime, a magic show by the Great Wizard, a ballet, and finally a masked ball, which was to continue all the second night into a third day.

The masked ball degenerated into a very wild affair early in the morning of March 5, 1856. Anderson, utterly at the end of his patience, ordered the lights turned off to end the revel, hoping that the mob would grope its way out. But nobody had to grope.

Covent Garden was illuminated with a flickery, uncertain

glow that suddenly materialized into tongues of flame. The great hall was on fire. Only the fortunate extinguishing of the lights enabled the revellers to gain enough warning to reach safety. By the time they did, the hall was an inferno. As in Glasgow, Anderson watched from a distance while the fire destroyed his entire collection of magical apparatus.

This time, however, Anderson was insured. Soon after the fire, he obtained and built new apparatus, intending to regain whatever losses the insurance had failed to cover. It was lucky that he invested in the equipment, for soon afterward, the Royal British Bank failed, wiping out all his fortune.

Since Anderson still had a magic show, he embarked upon another tour; this time Australia was his destination. He took his entire family with him. The tour proved a great success, though bad financial arrangements prevented him from receiving his proper share of the profits. He started back to England by way of the United States, where he arranged a tour from Washington to New Orleans, but he had just reached Richmond, Virginia, when the bombardment of Fort Sumter began the Civil War.

Anderson's billing, the "Wizard of the North," was the worst that he could possibly have chosen for appearances in the South. Even his name was against him, for the Union officer defending Fort Sumter was Major Anderson. Instead of realizing a profit, Anderson found his engagements canceled and his posters torn down. He returned to the Northern states and stayed there two years, hoping the war would end, but as it continued and business grew worse, he finally went back to England.

There, Anderson again attempted to retrieve his fortune. After a series of ups and downs, he experienced some success in the provincial halls and theaters, where he was still remembered. He continued performing until his sixtieth year, when, on the verge of a final farewell tour, he died on February 3, 1874, while playing an engagement in Darlington, England.

Professor Anderson was unquestionably the most famous magician of his day, for his name was known from the northern climes of Russia to the Australian bush. At one time or another, he performed in every theater in Great Britain and Ireland, as well as all the largest halls in the United States.

He appeared in palaces prepared for the occasion and in tents pitched to receive the crowds that sought to witness his performances. When time allowed, he built theaters to accommodate his audiences. A master of superlatives, his own title topped them all: Professor Anderson, the Great Wizard of the North.

Chapter 3

HERRMANN THE GREAT

(1843–1896)

The man in the gold-braided uniform leaned forward, his smooth chin resting in his cupped hand as he watched the magician perform the concluding number of his manipulative program. Not a move escaped the observer's dark eyes, and when the small but elegant group applauded the climax, his gaze remained fixed and his features immobile.

Yet when the magician had put away his props and was invited to join the gathering, the first to extend congratulations was the attentive personage with the gold braid and epaulets, whose green jacket gleamed with decorations that included an imperial star. He opened a box brought by an attendant, and from it took a magnificent gold watch, which he presented to the magician as a memento of the occasion.

The pleased performer accepted the gift with a profound bow, while the surrounding dignitaries joined in new applause. Such was the tribute of Napoleon Bonaparte, Emperor of the French, to Samuel Herrmann, the brilliant young magician who had just entertained the imperial court.

There was a special reason for Herrmann's skill. His were the hands of a surgeon, for medicine was his profession. He had taken up sleight of hand as an avocation, attracting so much notice among the elite of Paris that the emperor had wanted to see him perform. Samuel Herrmann continued to present magic following that triumph, and taught much of his art to his son Carl, who was born in 1816. But gradually, his medical practice demanded more of his time and he eventually abandoned magic almost entirely.

At his father's urging, Carl studied medicine, but the lure of legerdemain predominated in his case. Carl left school, joined a company of actors, and practiced ventriloquism along with magic, becoming a remarkable imitator of bird calls. After interrupting his new career to complete his service in the French army, Carl began touring with his own show, and by the age of thirty was recognized as one of Europe's most accomplished magicians.

In 1848, Carl Herrmann arrived in London and appeared at the Haymarket Theatre, presenting such up-to-date mysteries as the "Inexhaustible Bottle," the "Aerial Suspension," "Second Sight" and the production of fish bowls while wearing evening clothes. This was early in the year, prior to the arrival of Robert-Houdin, who performed those same marvels, claiming them as his own invention. Carl Herrmann billed himself as the "Premier Prestidigitateur of France," a title which Robert-Houdin felt was his own, so their rivalry was indeed keen.

Two years later, Carl Herrmann gave entertainments in Germany, Austria, Italy and Portugal, where he was decorated by the king and became the Chevalier Herrmann. He used that title from then on. In 1853, his superb skill gained him access to the select circles in Vienna, and he made that city his home, but he was almost as well known everywhere he went. His austere air, his large mustache and full beard gave him a distinguished appearance that enabled him to turn mere tricks into seeming miracles, but it was in the daring of his deceptions that his true greatness lay.

After producing four bowls of water, larger than those used by any other magicians, Carl Herrmann would go down into the audience and invite spectators to prod his arms and sides, and even frisk his long coattails. Those were the places from which the bowls had come, so anyone who suspected it would naturally assume that there could be no more. But from the very same cloth, the magician would promptly produce a fifth bowl, which had been nestling serenely in the hollow of his back.

At a special children's performance, Carl Herrmann magically filled a huge bowl with candy, which he distributed among the audience; then, from the empty bowl, he reeled out a few hundred yards of colored paper ribbons. Finally, gathering these and spreading them asunder, he produced four live geese from the cackling mass. Magicians witnessing this were more amazed than the audience, for they recognized that it depended upon Carl's ability at concealing objects about his tall, gaunt frame.

Carl Herrmann was always the magician, off the stage as well as on. Five minutes after joining a group, he would borrow a hat, show it empty, then proceed to extract a variety of articles belonging to persons present. The courteous chevalier had neatly filched the items from people's pockets, palmed them from sight, and secretly loaded them into the hat. His skill, coupled with surprise, made the productions seem truly magical.

On special occasions, Carl Herrmann had a way of planning fantastic surprises in advance. While performing in Madrid, he was invited to the home of a Spanish marquis, Don Mariano del Prado. When the guests were arriving, the marquis announced that he had hoped to provide partridges for dinner, but was unable to obtain them at that season.

No sooner said, than the Chevalier Herrmann borrowed the highest hat available, twirled it between his deft hands, and out flew two of the finest partridges that the marquis had ever seen. No one realized that Carl had made quiet inquiries regarding the marquis and had learned that his host was fond of partridges, but had been vainly trying to find some. Carl had sent away for a pair in time to have them on the appointed day. The mere mention of partridges was his cue to produce them magically.

In 1853, Carl Herrmann returned to Paris and was welcomed

by his father and other members of the family, which by then included sixteen children, of whom Carl was the eldest. At the time, Carl's youngest brother, Alexander, was only ten years of age, but he had already shown an interest in magic. He was so bright and handsome that Carl took him along to St. Petersburg to serve as a page boy in a command performance before the Czar of Russia.

This was done without the knowledge of Samuel Herrmann, for Carl's father had never quite forgiven him for taking up magic instead of medicine. For Alexander to suffer the same fate was just too much, and Samuel Herrmann was ready to go to any extreme to have his youngest son brought back, even to bringing kidnap charges against Carl. Fortunately, a compromise was reached, and Alexander was allowed to stay with Carl until they closed the tour and reached Vienna; then the boy was sent home to Paris.

Meanwhile, Carl had cannily been teaching advanced sleights to Alexander, including some of the manipulations that Carl himself had learned from their father. Alexander displayed his new skill to Samuel Herrmann, who was so impressed by the boy's aptitude that he decided to let him continue in magic, with Carl as his mentor. So Alexander returned to Vienna, on Carl's promise to give him a good education in other subjects besides magic.

Carl did, but magic came first. Alexander went with Carl on nearly every tour, working first as an assistant, and later doing part of the show himself. When they came to the United States in 1860, Alexander had developed a skill rivaling that of his famous brother. They appeared together at the Academy of Music in Brooklyn; then, with the outbreak of the Civil War, they left the United States and set out on a tour of Central and South America.

A few years later they separated and Alexander appeared on his own, until he again joined Carl in Vienna in 1867. They toured the United States together, and implanted the name Herrmann quite firmly there; then they once more went their individual ways, each with his own show. Carl, or Compars Herrmann, as he was also known, returned to play the capitals of Europe, while Alexander arrived in London in 1871 and opened an engagement at Egyptian Hall that lasted for one thousand and one nights.

By then, Alexander, though resembling Carl, had developed a distinct and magnetic personality of his own. His keen eyes, imposing mustache and goatee gave him a satanic appearance which greatly impressed his audiences. Due to the twenty-seven years' difference in age between the two Herrmanns, they belonged to different generations. Many persons supposed that Carl was Alexander's uncle, rather than his brother, and there were even rumors that they were not related, but that Alexander was simply an assistant whom Carl had groomed to become his successor.

Such stories gained currency from the fact that Carl retired from the stage before Alexander completed his three-year triumph at Egyptian Hall. It was supposed that Alexander would tour Europe next, but in the financial panic of 1873, Carl met with reverses and was forced to leave Vienna and return to magic to regain his fortune. By the next year, Carl was making many appearances in European cities where he was already well known.

Alexander left the European field to Carl and set out to tour the United States. On the boat, he met a dancer named Adelaide Scarsez, whom he married in 1875. In America, Alexander revived the name of Herrmann so successfully that he decided to stay there. In 1876, he became a naturalized American citizen. Increasing the size of his show year by year and profiting in the same proportion, he became known as Herrmann the Great.

Between tours Herrmann lived in a fine mansion at White-stone, Long Island. There, his yacht, the *Diavolo*, was moored in Long Island Sound, ready to steam into New York harbor and pick up friends who arrived from Europe. His private car stood on a siding at the Whitestone depot, along with two baggage cars to carry his equipment—which included a pair of horses and a carriage—whenever he went out on tour.

As for his performance, Alexander Herrmann completely enthralled his audience with his opening act, as will be apparent from this firsthand description recorded by a famous magician of a later day, the Great Raymond, who was so impressed by Herrmann's routine that he remembered it in detail:

> Herrmann opened the act by vanishing his gloves, which in his hands seemed delightfully real. Then, he ran his fingers lightly over his wand and from the end squeezed an orange. He followed this with a trick known as the "Cone, Orange and Rice" which was one of his favorites and very effective. That concluded, he casually showed his hands empty, and from behind his right knee, he plucked a fanned pack of cards.
>
> Next, he presented a series of card tricks depending on pure sleight-of-hand and misdirection, terminating with the rising cards from a glass goblet on a small table near the footlights. After the selected cards had risen, Herrmann took the pack from the goblet, tossed them in the air and they were gone. Apparently, he was through with cards—but, no, his empty hands were suddenly filled with them! These, he scaled over the audience to the topmost row in the gallery.
>
> Herrmann then borrowed a silk hat—top hats were common in those days—and performed the "Miser's Dream," catching a surprising number of silver dollars from the air. These were poured clankingly from the hat into a silver tray, displayed to the audience, and dumped into a paper bag which was wrapped up and tossed to the owner of the hat who found that the silver dollars had changed into a box of candy!
>
> A piece of paper remained over from the packaging

process, so Herrmann casually rolled it into a ball and knocked it through his knee, then tossed it in the air, where it disappeared. Many surprising things were then discovered in the hat—enough to fill a small trunk!—and after thanking the owner of the hat, Herrmann started to return it and discovered a rabbit in it.

Herrman stroked the rabbit and suddenly pulled it apart by the ears. Lo and behold, he had two rabbits, one in each hand. He put the rabbits on a table and called attention to the fact that both were the same size. Then, he scooped them up from the table and the two became one. He pointed out that this rabbit was much fatter, so he suddenly seized a pistol from the table, tossed the rabbit in the air, shot at it, and the rabbit was gone!

Rushing down the runway into the audience, Herrmann pulled the vanished rabbit from the coat of an astounded spectator. During that action, the curtains closed in one. Herrmann returned to the stage and stood in front of the curtain, talking to the rabbit as he cradled it in his arms. The bunny turned its head toward Herrmann and cocked up one ear, causing much laughter and more applause. Exit Herrmann—a roll of drums—music crescendo.

The curtains parted and Madame Herrmann appeared in her colorful serpentine and fire dances. At the finish her voluminous white silk dress apparently caught on fire and she danced in flames, a beautiful woman apparently being consumed by fire. Thus ended the first part of Herrmann's program.

Smoothly routined though Herrmann's opening was, it could go wrong at times; and that was when the real test came. In this opening and others that were more elaborate, Herrmann had "loads" consisting of everything from cards and flowers to live rabbits and strings of handkerchiefs, all placed where he needed them. If he slipped on one, he could cover it with the next, so he never was seriously discommoded—except on one occasion.

It was a warm evening and Herrmann was seated in his shirt sleeves in his dressing room, chatting with the theater manager, who left just before the curtain call. Herrmann had already loaded his full-dress coat, so he slid into it carefully, smoothed the sleeves while leaving the dressing room and strode on stage, putting on his gloves. But the moment he started to remove them, he realized that something was wrong.

He wasn't wearing his own coat!

That spelled disaster for the first act. Another magician might have stood there, wondering whether to walk off or ring down the curtain, but not Herrmann the Great. Casually, he laid his gloves aside, picked up a pack of cards that were fortunately on the table and began a few fancy flourishes.

All the while, he was wondering about his coat, and suddenly he had the answer. The manager, too, was wearing a full-dress suit. He must have taken the magician's coat by mistake.

With that, Herrmann gave the pack a final flourish, snapped his fingers toward the wing to bring an assistant onstage, and began to sail cards into the audience. As the assistant arrived, Herrmann undertoned: "Find the manager! He's wearing my coat! And bring me more packs of cards!"

The assistant left, and came on with a few packs of cards, saying that he'd sent someone to look for the manager. Herrmann began to scale the new packs, and told the assistant to bring him still more cards. He was speeding cards to the balcony, straight to hands that waved for them, and the audience was getting excited over his remarkable aim. Additional packs were rushed onstage by the assistant, who brought news that they were still trying to find the manager. Herrmann now was sizzling the cards to the far reaches of the gallery more accurately than ever.

73

Then, when the spare packs were almost used up, with Herrmann nearly exhausted and the audience in a wild frenzy, the surprised manager appeared at the wing. Herrmann scaled a last batch of cards and bowed off to tumultuous applause for the greatest card-throwing act ever seen. Offstage, he hastily removed the manager's coat, peeled his own from the man's back, made a quick check of the contents, and strode onstage again, bowing to a new burst of applause as he went into his original routine.

Many other tales have been told of Herrmann's quick wit in lesser emergencies. In one of his tricks, he used an egg, which was handily tucked beneath his vest, ready to be palmed when needed. In performing a preliminary card trick, Herrmann sprang the pack from hand to hand and brushed his vest with his forearm. The egg slipped loose and broke on the stage, catching the audience's immediate attention.

Herrmann saw it, too, and raised his head with a triumphant smile as he gestured from the egg to the cards that were in his other hand, and announced: "Wonderful! An egg from a pack of cards!"

Once, when he was producing his bowls of goldfish from beneath his coat, the rubber cover slipped from the first one, and instead of remaining hidden in the cloth, fell to the stage. That could be very bad, for if people wondered what it was, they might begin to guess when the other bowls appeared.

Herrmann didn't let them wonder. He laid the first bowl aside, stooped, and picked up the rubber cover. Then he spread it and put it on his head, saying: "Ah, you see? An artist's beret. I always wear one when I do this trick." With that, he went right on producing fish bowls, but without letting any more "berets" drop. At the finish, he took off the one that he was wearing and tossed it aside as he bowed to the applause.

Sometimes Herrmann finished the first act with a big illusion, but most of his larger effects were performed in later portions of the show, which had as many as four acts. The showmanship that characterized his sleights was equally apparent in the illusions.

The "Escape from Sing Sing" was one of Herrmann's most sensational mysteries, and it served as a pattern for many later illusions. Few of these, however, were as effective as the original presentation, which was artfully designed to combine audience appeal with ingenious deception.

The curtain rose to disclose the gray-walled interior of a prison, with two square cells standing well apart. Each cell was slightly over four feet square and more than six feet high. Top and bottom were solid, but the walls—including the door at the front—were composed simply of upright steel bars, a half a dozen to a side, while the corners were a thin framework.

Herrmann walked around the empty cell at the left, calling attention to red spring blinds at the top of each side, though he did not draw them down—as yet. Instead, he came from behind the cell and walked over to the cell on the right and showed that it, too, was empty, and equipped with similar blinds. In the course of this, there was a commotion at the wing and a convict attired in stripes came dashing on the stage.

Herrmann quickly drew his magician's revolver, halted the convict and forced him into the cell on the right, clanging the barred door to keep him there. Herrmann then circled the cell, drawing down the red blinds, while a voice from inside began shouting, "Let me out! Let me out!"

With a show of surprise, Herrmann raised the blinds of the right-hand cell, and in place of the convict, the audience saw a uniformed guard. Otherwise, the cell was empty, its thin floor and top offering scarcely enough space to hide a costume, if the man had switched from his convict's stripes. But while the spectators were thinking along that line, there came a shout from the audience and the missing convict rushed down the aisle and up onto the stage!

75

By then, Herrmann had released the guard and they grabbed the convict when he arrived. During the struggle, people saw that the guard was shorter and more heavy-set than the convict, which ruled out any notion of a costume switch. What followed flabbergasted the audience even more. Between them, Herrmann and the guard thrust the convict into the cell on the left and hurriedly drew down the blinds on both cells.

Then, with cool deliberation, Herrmann fired his revolver at the cell on the left. The blinds flew up, showing open bars on every side. The convict was gone again! Turning about, Herrmann fired at the cell on the right, up went its blinds, and there was the escaped prisoner back in the cell from which he had originally vanished!

Herrmann brought the convict from the cell and they took a bow; then Herrmann walked forward alone and the curtain fell on the Sing Sing scene, while the magician took another bow at the footlights.

Now to reveal the subtle craft behind the Sing Sing sensation: The prison scene was chosen because it justified cabinets shaped like cells, as well as a dull gray background suggesting the stone walls of a jail. There were red blinds at the front and sides of each cell, but at the back—just beyond the bars—was a gray blind matching the rear curtain. When these were down, the audience still thought they saw clear to the prison wall, for the intervening bars made the illusion perfect.

At the outset, all blinds were up on the cell at the left, so Herrmann walked completely around it, testing the red blinds. But the back blind was down in the cell on the right, and on a narrow shelf-like projection behind it stood a stubby assistant in the uniform of a prison guard. In showing that cell empty, Herrmann came in front of it while calling attention to the red blinds.

When the convict suddenly dashed onstage, Herrmann forced him into the cabinet on the right and drew the red blinds. The guard immediately raised the back blind and switched places with the convict through a set of loose bars. As soon as the convict drew down the back blind, the guard began to shout. Herrmann promptly raised the red blinds to reveal the guard.

That was the cue for a second convict to come dashing down the aisle. The double was the same height as the original prisoner and their striped garb made them appear identical. The double was promptly parked in the empty cell at the left. As soon as its red blinds were drawn, he stepped out beyond the movable bars and drew down the back blind, while Herrmann and the guard were drawing down the blinds on the right-hand cell.

A pistol shot at the cell on the left—bang!—the convict was gone. His counterpart, meanwhile, had raised the back blind of the right-hand cell and had stepped inside, where he was immediately discovered. While Herrmann and the original convict were taking their bow, the guard strolled off behind the cell on the right, which was now entirely open, drawing attention from the left-hand cell, where a man was still behind the lowered back blind.

One season, Herrmann's famous stage manager, Billy Robinson, was acting as the double. Just before the Sing Sing illusion, Robinson would put on a convict's outfit and go out through the stage alley and around to the front of the house, timing it so that he would arrive there just after the original convict was transformed into the guard. One night, however, Robinson did not appear from the audience as expected.

Herrmann stalled as long as he could gracefully; then, rising to the emergency as he always did, he motioned the guard into the cell on the left, gave him undertoned instructions, and lowered the red blinds. The guard moved to the back, Herrmann fired a shot, and the red blinds flew up. The guard, like the convict, was gone, leaving both cells apparently empty. Herrmann stepped forward with a bow and as the curtains closed in behind him, he addressed the audience:

"You ask where they have gone? Listen, and I shall tell

you." His face gleamed with his most knowing smile, as he said, "Back to Sing Sing, where they both came from."

Herrmann was almost right about Robinson. While turning the corner in his convict's uniform, Billy had run into a policeman who was patrolling his beat. The officer had promptly taken him into custody and dragged him away despite his protest that he wasn't a convict, but was working in Herrmann's show.

At the station house, the desk sergeant was also skeptical, but listened long enough to ask why he was wearing the stripes. When Robinson tried to explain that he was playing a part in the "Escape from Sing Sing," the sergeant took it as an admission of guilt.

Robinson was slapped into a real jail cell to be shipped back to the penitentiary, but by the time the show was over at the theater, Herrmann was really worried about his missing stage manager. Thinking that Robinson might have met with an accident and gone to a hospital, Herrmann went to the police station to report him missing. There, all was happily explained and Robinson was released.

Herrmann always liked to give an illusion a timely theme. For the mystery entitled "Vanity Fair," he used the popular song of the season, "After the Ball," and Madame Herrmann, attired in an evening gown, waltzed onstage to its dreamy strains. A wide full-length mirror was wheeled about so that the audience could see all sides. It was then set well back near the center of the stage, allowing its surface to be viewed clearly from every angle. The mirror was in a large ornamental frame mounted on legs so that people could see beneath it. Curtains extended from the sides to create a boudoir atmosphere, and a sheet of thick plate glass, supported by metal brackets, formed a projecting platform a few feet above the bottom frame. Madame Herrmann finished her dance by ascending a short flight of steps to reach the platform, and the steps were taken away.

While the orchestra softly continued its theme, the lady of the occasion admired herself in the mirror. Then Herrmann and an assistant approached with a large folding screen. They set the screen about the lady, but the mirror was so much larger that portions of its surface were constantly visible, at top, sides or bottom, leaving absolutely no way for Madame Herrmann to leave the isolated platform where she was hidden by the screen.

The music grew louder, and with the final notes of the captivating waltz, Herrmann and his assistant whisked away the screen and flattened it. Truly "the ball was over," for not only was the music ended, but the lady herself was completely gone, leaving the surface of the mirror as blank as if she had dissolved into its silvery sheen.

Here was indeed a riddle to amaze the skeptical observers who talked of tricks being "done with mirrors." In this case, a mirror had been openly used to prove that trickery was impossible. When it was wheeled around and off the stage, disclosing no trace of the vanished lady, the spectators felt they had seen everything. And so they had—except for the part that they were not supposed to see.

The mirror actually filled the frame, as the onlookers supposed; but the portion below the glass platform was fronted by a smaller section that appeared to be part of the big mirror, but really masked it. Behind that, there was a rectangular opening in the main mirror, just about the width of the screen.

Once the screen was in place, the big mirror was pushed upward, like a window, but its motion was not discernible. The upper edge slid into a high ornamental extension at the top of the frame. The lower edge was hidden by the masking mirror beneath the platform, and this action brought the rectangular opening up behind the screen. The lady slid through that space and reached a narrow ramp that was extended through a secret opening in the backdrop to the

79

platform. She was drawn backstage, the ramp was removed and the mirror was lowered, unnoticed, to its original position.

The curtains extending from the sides of the mirror prevented people in the side aisles or the boxes from seeing in back of the frame while the illusion was in progress. But there was nothing suspicious about them, and the fact that the mirror was set so near the backdrop did not detract from the mystery. It had to be well back for everyone to view it properly, and since the mirror represented an apparently impassable barrier, the mystery was complete.

Another of Herrmann's larger effects was the "Noah's Ark" illusion. A replica of Noah's famous ark, supported on two trestles, was placed in the center of the stage. The ark was actually a large, oblong cabinet, with curtained windows set in its front, but it had two ornamental extensions, one at each end, giving it a resemblance to a double-prowed ship.

Herrmann and his assistants promptly proved that the ark was not yet occupied, for they lowered the front and back, raised the top like a lid, and even swung down the ornamental prows to show that nothing was concealed behind them. Then the ark was closed, the prows raised, and moments later birds and animals emerged from the windows. The animals, though mostly dogs and cats, were made up to resemble elephants and tigers in miniature, adding to the exotic atmosphere.

For a finale, the front of the cabinet was lowered, revealing a girl in an ancient costume reclining within, as the last tenant of the ark. Her appearance was quite a surprise, considering the large number of creatures that had already been produced.

The "Noah's Ark" was a self-contained illusion, in which everything was already packed in place, yet due to ingenious design and well-rehearsed presentation, the average spectator was lulled into believing that the contrivance was quite empty. The girl was strapped to the inside of the back door, and when the front and back were lowered, allowing the audience

LA CORNE D'ABONDANCE

LE GARDE-FRANÇAISE

LE PATISSIER DU PALAIS-ROYAL

LA PENDULE AÉRIENNE

(Coll. Serge)

DIAVOLO-ANTONIO, le voltigeur au trapèze

A portrait of Robert-Houdin and some of his principal mysteries, indicating his leaning toward automata and mechanical marvels rather than the more spectacular magical effects of his contemporaries.

A poster showing Robert-Houdin's "Plume Production" with his full stage set as background and his older son, Emile, as his assistant. The four plumes in his left hand were produced from his sleeves, followed by a dozen from beneath his vest. The latter quantity has been purposely exaggerated.

An illustration from *Modern Magic* by Professor Hoffmann, showing the construction and working of the "Pyramids of Egypt" as performed by Robert-Houdin in his first real show.

An invitation to Robert-Houdin's theater issued by his brother-in-law, Hamilton, who succeeded him as director and main performer.

John Henry Anderson, the "Wizard of the North," at the age of thirty-seven.

Alexander Herrmann, aptly known as "Herrmann the Great,"
who raised modern magic to a new peak of artistry.

MUSIC HALL, LEEDS.

GRAND FINAL FAREWELL WEEK
of
THE GREAT WIZARD!

FIVE NIGHTS ONLY!
PROFESSOR ANDERSON,
THE LAST TIME FOR EVER IN LEEDS!

Positively the last Five Nights of Wonders!
Unalterably the last Five Nights of Magic!
Definitively the last Five Nights of Incomprehensibilities!
Irrevocably the last Five Nights of the Wizard of Wizards!

Monday, Oct. 16th; Tuesday, Oct. 17th; (No Performance on Wednesday;)
Thursday, Oct. 19th; Friday, Oct. 20th; Saturday, Oct. 21st.

An Anderson "Farewell" program. The master showman utilized these to swell the box-office returns in the closing days of many engagements.

Adelaide Herrmann, early in her career, when she assisted
Alexander at the Eden Theater in Paris.

Carl "Compars" Herrmann (left), Alexander's brother, tutor, and predecessor; and Leon Herrmann (right), Alexander's nephew and successor to the title of "Herrmann the Great."

Leon Herrmann performing the "Obedient Ball." A hidden assistant operated a cord running to the base, actuating a tiny lever set in a narrow slot in the back of the upright rod. This caused the ball to rise and fall in answer to the audience's questions.

Kellar in his early days, shortly after completing his world tour.

The Kellar of later years, as thousands of mystified Americans remembered him; genial in manner, baffling in wizardry.

PRESENTING HIS LATEST AND GREATEST WONDER "GONE"

The two steps of Kellar's "Gone" illusion are depicted in this poster, "before" and "after" the vanish. The space below the table was actually hidden by forty-five-degree mirrors, a standard device of the period, enabling the lady to "disappear" through an unsuspected trap.

East meets West. Kellar, the dean of American magicians, greeting Ching Ling Foo, the original Chinese conjuror.

William E. Robinson, the "Man of Mystery" and his wife, "Dot,"
as they appeared in their early career as American performers.

The "Half Lady" illusion, based on the "Black Art" principle that Robinson introduced into many of his stage illusions. The lower illustration reveals the secret.

A 1905 poster of Thurston in his first illusion act, presenting the "Inexhaustible Coconut Shell" in its original form. The water streaming from his raised left hand is an artist's exaggeration of the effect.

Thurston presenting his famous "Floating Lady" with Fernanda Myra as "Princess Karnac."

Thurston hypnotizing a Hindu for the "Living Burial," which duplicated the feats of Oriental fakirs.

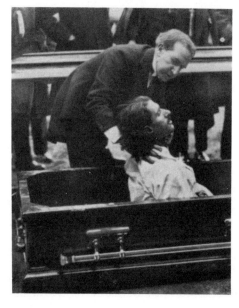

One of Hardeen's posters, showing him performing his most sensational escapes.

Houdini being lowered into the "Water Torture Cell," from which he escaped after the stocks encasing his ankles were pad-locked to the cell.

Houdini about to jump from a diving board, shackled with a ball and chain, from which he escaped while under water.

One of the most striking of Houdini's portraits, emphasizing his dynamic personality.

to see through the cabinet, the back door was dropped a split-second sooner, so the girl was hanging out of sight before the front door fell.

The top was quite innocent, so special attention was given to it; and meanwhile, the ornamental ends, which looked like mere flaps, were dropped downward behind the front door. They contained secret compartments stocked with birds and animals. The ark was brought back to its original condition, the various creatures were released and swarmed over the stage, while the girl was produced last of all.

As a preliminary, the ark was sometimes filled with water to add to the mystery. The water, which was poured from buckets into the top of the ark, simply went down through a pipe in a leg of one of the trestles and was drained off below the stage.

The three illusions just described illustrate the wide variety of Herrmann's methods. In the "Escape from Sing Sing," a special mode of concealment was used, coupled with speed and surprise; in "Vanity Fair" there was slow motion and a complete getaway; in "Noah's Ark" ingenious construction was the answer.

Like his brother Carl, Alexander Herrmann was a magician offstage as well as on. When he was introduced to President Grant at the White House, he promptly produced a handful of cigars from the famous general's whiskers, and they proved to be Grant's favorite brand.

At dinner, after finishing a drink of wine, Herrmann would apparently toss the glass into the air, where it vanished. Later, he would borrow a napkin and produce the glass from its folds, or bring it from beneath a friend's coat. Even expert magicians were baffled by this deft feat, for Herrmann apparently showed his hands completely empty, and wherever the glass might have gone, there seemed no possible way for him to reclaim it, as he made no suspicious move.

Here, Herrmann's technique was remarkable. He palmed the stemmed glass by its base, turning the back of his hand toward the onlookers, as he pretended to give the glass a toss, which all eyes followed. Then he swung down to the dining table and stopped there, with the glass extending down below the edge while his fingers idly strummed the table in the fashion of a pianist's, a slightly impatient habit that he had purposely cultivated.

This was misdirection par excellence. Observers, thinking in terms of a tall glass, never pictured its base as the equivalent of a large coin, and just as easily palmed. The only problem was concealment of the extending goblet, and the table edge provided that. So natural, so habitual were Herrmann's moves that afterward people would swear he had shown both hands empty, back and front, immediately following the toss.

By picking up a napkin or reaching for someone's coat lapel with his free hand, Herrmann was able to slide his other hand beneath the table without anyone noticing and thus magically reclaim the palmed wineglass. At times, he began with a transparent celluloid disk in his free hand and used it to cap the moistened rim of a filled wineglass. He made the toss, and the glass vanished, wine and all, the disk retaining the liquid when the goblet was inverted. In bringing the glass from a napkin, Herrmann secretly removed the disk and later palmed it away.

Even more amazing was Herrmann's vanish of a large orange, a trick that he performed when about to leave the dinner table. As he vanished the orange with an upward toss, Herrmann immediately arose, brushed his hands and sleeves, showed his hands completely empty and strolled away, leaving no trace of the departed fruit.

For this mystery he utilized a device like a small knapsack beneath his coat. Elastic cords ran over his shoulders and under his arms, terminating in a circular wire frame with a loose cloth bag at the center of his back. Before vanishing the orange, Herrmann secretly drew the bag downward and forward, bringing it to the edge of the chair between his knees.

His seated weight, resting on the elastic cords, kept the device in place.

Herrmann gave the orange a preliminary toss, caught it near the table edge and dropped it while making a pretended toss exactly like the first. A tested and reliable deception, this carried eyes upward, most persons imagining that they saw the orange melt in mid-air. Instead, it dropped into the waiting bag. Before the surprise was over, Herrmann rose from his chair, letting the knapsack fly up beneath his coat, so that the orange nestled in the hollow of his back, its whereabouts unsuspected.

In the 1880s, Herrmann made a special tour of Europe and gave a command performance for Czar Alexander III of Russia. They made a striking contrast, the two Alexanders, monarchs of Magic and Muscovy respectively. Herrmann's skill impressed his Imperial Majesty, but the czar was a great believer in brute strength. He felt that as ruler of Russia, he should pack more physical power than even the roughest and most burly peasant in his realm.

The story goes that the czar demonstrated his strength for Herrmann by squaring a pack of cards and tearing it in half. He then handed the torn cards to the magician to see if his delicate touch could outmatch the czar's iron grip. It did that and more. Herrmann coolly placed one half on the other, squared them neatly, and tore them both together.

At the Eden Theater in Paris, Herrmann's performance was witnessed by the Prince and Princess of Wales, later to become King Edward VII and Queen Alexandra of England. It was there, in 1885, that Alexander met his brother Carl for the last time. Almost seventy, Carl was actually planning to retire again and was grooming their nephew, Leon Herrmann, to be his successor. This confirmed the informal arrangement whereby Carl was to appear exclusively in Europe and Alexander chiefly in America. Two years later, Carl died, but Alexander was quite content to let Leon take over in Europe. Alexander's own realm was profitable enough.

Only in America could anyone have increased his fame and fortune as did Herrmann the Great in the next ten years. His Whitestone mansion became a gathering place for the elite of the American theatrical world, who regarded Herrmann as one of their outstanding luminaries.

True, Herrmann lost much of what he made by aiding other actors in unfortunate theatrical ventures, for he was extremely generous. But he felt that the greatest period of his career was still ahead of him, and that he could always make more. Wherever he went, he was recognized; on the street, at hotels, in trains and trolleys. Always he was ready with a timely trick that enhanced his reputation and brought customers to the box office.

A typical day in Herrmann's strenuous life was Wednesday, December 16, 1896, when he was finishing a week's engagement at the Lyceum Theatre in Rochester, New York. He had invited a whole school to his matinee, and that afternoon the house was packed with such an enthusiastic throng that he extended the length of his performance.

Between then and the evening show, he learned that a theatrical troupe was stranded in Rochester, so he paid their bills, bought them tickets to New York and invited them to his evening show before they left. After the show, Herrmann was guest of honor at a banquet given by the Genesee Valley Club, and the fete lasted until well after midnight.

A group from the party accompanied Herrmann to his special train, which was leaving early in the morning for Bradford, Pennsylvania, a three-hour trip from Rochester. The last person to whom Herrmann said good-bye was the young dramatic critic of a Rochester newspaper, John Northern Hilliard, who later became America's foremost author on magic. Shortly before the the train reached Bradford, Herrmann was stricken with a heart attack in the stateroom of his private car. He failed to recover and that day, December 17, 1896, the world learned that Herrmann the Great was dead.

The public still clamored for his show, however, and Madame Herrmann sent to Europe for his nephew Leon, who was presenting some of Carl's specialties in vaudeville. Leon was a clever, capable performer, who closely resembled Alexander, though he was shorter and less dynamic. But because he had spent much of his recent life in Paris, he lacked command of the English language and was unable to gauge the reactions of American audiences.

Despite Leon's skill and vivacity, the Herrmann show began to decline. The audiences unquestionably missed Alexander and his inimitable style; also, Kellar, who had already furnished keen competition to Alexander, was gaining in popularity. After a few seasons Madame Herrmann decided to present her own show, and appeared as "the Queen of Magic," becoming the first woman magician in the history of the art.

Leon turned to vaudeville and presented a sparkling act with a small group of assistants and his wife Marie as his leading lady. He capitalized on his uncle's fame by billing himself as Herrmann the Great, but after touring the United States for a few more seasons, he returned to France. There he suffered a brief illness and died on May 17, 1909, at the age of forty-two.

However, Madame Adelaide Herrmann continued performing. She also took advantage of the increasing popularity of vaudeville and condensed her show into a headline attraction entitled "A Night in Japan." For twenty-five years she performed graceful sleights, colorful effects and intriguing illusions, such as the "Aerial Suspension" and "Noah's Ark," until a disastrous fire destroyed much of her cherished apparatus.

Rather than rebuild her show, "the Queen of Magic" retired from the stage. She died a few years later, on February 19, 1932, at the age of seventy-five, and with her passing, the magical name of Herrmann became a memory.

85

Chapter 4

KELLAR

(1849–1922)

The eleven-year-old boy was tired as he trudged the last quarter-mile along the dusty road outside of Buffalo, New York. He was worried, too. Nervously he glanced at the crumpled newspaper ad that he carried in his hand. It read:

WANTED:

BOY TO WORK AS ASSISTANT
FOR THE FAKIR OF AVA.

That advertisement was several days old, and by now the job was probably filled. If so, the boy had come for nothing. But he kept on past a pair of iron gates, toward an imposing house, where a small black-and-tan dog came bounding toward him. The boy was patting the dog, which was responding with appreciative whines, when an austere man with a broad mustache and a tiny goatee stepped out on the veranda.

He was Isaiah Harris Hughes, the famous magician who called himself the Fakir of Ava. He inquired if the boy had come for the job and when the boy nodded, Hughes asked his name. The boy gave it: "Harry Keller." Smilingly, Hughes told him that the job was his, for a very simple reason. Dozens of boys had already applied, but the little dog had snapped and snarled at all of them, until Hughes had decided that he would hire the first boy that the dog liked. That happened to be young Harry Keller.

The terms amounted to a few dollars a month, with room, board and traveling expenses included, all that a boy could want around the time of the American Civil War. From the outset, young Harry reveled in the job, for he was promptly taken backstage in the barn, where he was rehearsed in the working of the magical equipment that had been set up there.

It was a still greater thrill when they started on the road a few weeks later and Harry found himself sharing the stage with the renowned Fakir of Ava, who despite his Oriental title, performed in the conventional full-dress attire of the modern magician.

Originally, the fakir had worn Oriental robes in order to produce fish bowls and other bulky items, and to give himself an aura of mystery that was new to American audiences. But as his technique improved and new methods were invented, he discarded the robes and changed his style of performance. Already famous as the Fakir of Ava, he retained that title, and his remarkable switch from East to West proved a great advertisement for his show.

At the time when he hired young Harry, the self-styled Fakir of Ava was in his fifties and had put away a tidy fortune. He was touring territory that he knew was profitable, and intended to retire after several years more. When Harry asked him if he intended to go back to Ava, the fakir smiled and said that he had never been there. He had chosen the remote Burmese city as his pretended birthplace because he was confident that he would never meet anyone who knew enough about the place to cross-examine him, and so far, he never had.

Harry enjoyed hearing the fakir's tales of wizardry while they waited at railroad junctions, rode cross-country in stagecoaches, or sat in comfortable hotel rooms between shows. But sharing the stage with the renowned fakir was even more wonderful. It was Harry's job to go down into the audience and borrow a hat into which the fakir tossed coins that he plucked out of the air; later the hat was used for cooking a magic omelet. Harry also asked for rings and watches, which the magician vanished in various ways and caused to reappear in equally mysterious fashion.

During off-hours, Harry practiced the coin-catching himself. Known both as the "Aerial Treasury" and the "Miser's Dream," the trick was simple in principle. From his pocket or a table, the magician secretly picked up a stack of twenty or more half-dollars, which he held cupped in the fingers of his left hand as he reached with his right hand to receive the borrowed hat. This was always a high hat of stiff material, a common type in those days; but in later years, magicians usually borrowed derby hats, which answered just as well.

Under cover of the hat, the magician placed the fingers of his left hand inside the brim, pressing the coins against the band, while he extended his thumb over the brim to gain a grip there. With his right hand, he reached in the air and pretended to throw a coin into the hat, at the same time releasing the lowermost of the hidden coins. This landed in the hat with an audible plunk and the magician promptly brought it out with his right hand and triumphantly displayed it to the audience.

Then came the real deception. In pretending to drop the coin back in the hat, the magician actually palmed it in his right hand, but let a coin plunk from his left instead. He reached into the air once again, this time showing the palmed coin at his finger tips, and repeated the pretended throw into the hat. Continuing thus, he apparently plucked coin after coin from the atmosphere, until the hat was jingling with the accumulated wealth. In showing the contents, some magicians displayed the hat with the right hand, enabling the left to obtain another stack of coins so the "catch" could be continued.

The Fakir of Ava also performed a watch trick in which he placed a borrowed timepiece in a small mortar of the type used by druggists, where he apparently pounded it to pieces with a stubby rod, or pestle. The real watch slid out through a secret opening into the fakir's hand, while chunks of metal, glass and broken works were released from within the hollow pestle, to pass as the smashed watch.

The fakir then stepped offstage to get a gun; in that moment, he slipped the watch to his young assistant. While the fakir loaded the pistol with the mass of junk and added a charge of powder, Harry hooked the real watch onto the back of a target that he brought onstage. The fakir fired the pistol, and the watch appeared completely restored, in the exact center of the target.

The standard "Watch Target" had a reversible "bull's-eye" that flipped about, but the Fakir of Ava used an improved type that was set beforehand so the pull of a thread would instantly bring the watch into sight. All went well until one night when Harry found that the release was already tripped. There wasn't any way to set the target again, nor even to tell the fakir what was wrong, so Harry grabbed an envelope that was lying on a table, held the watch behind it and came onstage, loudly announcing that he had a telegram for a member of the audience.

From the odd name that Harry called, the fakir knew something was up, so he waited while his assistant went through the audience with the envelope. Naturally, Harry found no takers, but in the course of his pretended mission, he managed to slip the watch into a spectator's pocket. When he came up on the stage, he handed the telegram to the fakir and whispered where the watch really was.

The fakir fired at the target, but no watch appeared there. Feigning annoyance, he told the audience that his assistant's stupid interruption had disturbed the prevailing spirits and put them in a prankish mood. He then said that he would use a "spirit bell" to locate the watch. This was a small glass dome topped by a metal ring which hung on a hook extending from an upright stand. The bell had an outside arm with a clapper that answered questions by bonging once for "Yes" and twice for "No."

Actually, Harry operated the bell from backstage by pulling a cord that ran down through the stand and forced a pin up from the hook into a corresponding hole in the ring above the glass bell. That, in turn, actuated the clapper, enabling Harry to ring answers to the fakir's queries, which he heard offstage. When the magician asked if the watch had flown into the audience, the bell bonged once; next, the "spirits" counted to the exact seat and row where an astonished spectator found the watch in his own pocket.

After several seasons, Harry decided to start out as a magician on his own. He soon changed the spelling of his name to Kellar, to distinguish himself from Heller, a noted magician of the time. But it was hard for a newcomer to succeed, so he took a temporary job as an assistant with the Davenport Brothers, a pair of mystery workers who convinced great crowds of gullible persons that they were genuine spirit mediums.

The two brothers, Ira Erastus and William Henry, put on a very remarkable act in which they utilized a large cabinet with three full-size doors set in a row. The cabinet was mounted on trestles, proving there was no access to the stage beneath. The brothers seated themselves at opposite ends of the cabinet and each was firmly tied to his chair with stout ropes by a committee of volunteers from the audience.

Bells, tambourines and a guitar were placed in the center portion of the cabinet and all three doors were shut. A moment later, chaos broke loose. Loud raps were heard, tambourines were banged, bells were rung and the guitar was strummed. The doors suddenly flew open and the brothers were seen, still tied.

As soon as the doors were closed, the racket began again, and this time hands appeared in a diamond-shaped opening near the top of the center door. Bells and tambourines were flung out, but when the doors flew wide, the brothers were seen to be tied as firmly as before. A man chosen from the committee was then seated in the center section, and when the doors were closed the spirits really went wild. The stranger was flung from the center door, his coat gone, his necktie twisted about his leg, and a tambourine crowning his head.

The Davenports' secret was their ability to obtain slack while being tied. Each medium worked as follows: A man from the committee was told to tie a long piece of rope around the medium's left wrist, near the center, with the knots at the inside. The medium then put his hands behind his back, saying that he would place his right wrist across his left, so it could be tied in the same fashion.

However, when he turned his back, the medium drew one end of the rope between the first two fingers of his left hand, around in back of the second finger, and forward between the second and third fingers. He covered this loop with his right forearm as he placed his right wrist across the left. The right wrist was then tied as tightly as the left.

But once the door of the cabinet was closed, the medium simply bent his left second finger inward and released the loop, gaining the slack to free his right hand. Later, he reversed the process, regaining the loop so his wrists would again appear to be securely bound.

If unable to obtain such full slack, it was possible to work with less, but even if one Davenport should be securely tied, the other would be able to release himself and loosen his brother's bonds. On those occasions, the manifestations were slower in getting started, that was all. Sometimes, the Davenports varied their routine by winding up completely free. That, too, was attributed to the spirits, though the brothers never actually claimed such supernatural aid; they simply let people form their own conclusions.

The Davenports had taken on a partner named William Fay, so the act was known as the Brothers Davenport and Mr. Fay when Kellar joined it. By the time Kellar graduated from assistant to business manager, the Davenports had taught him their rope tie; and in 1874, Fay and Kellar made a trip through Mexico with their own show. This was so successful that Kellar, though only twenty-five years of age, made a still more ambitious tour of South America, where he appeared before Emperor Dom Pedro II, of Brazil, but he lost most of his profits in a bank failure.

Kellar still had enough money, however, to start out with a company called the Royal Illusionists, who opened a three-week engagement in San Francisco on May 15, 1876, and later headed westward on a tour of the Orient. Kellar's magical performance and his version of the Davenport cabinet act won him fame in many lands, and he even put on a command performance before King Thibaw of Burma, in the royal palace of Ava. Afterward, Kellar mailed a copy of the program to his old friend and tutor, Isaiah Hughes, who had retired and was living comfortably in his home near Buffalo.

Though Kellar's travels were a success, his great goal was to present his own big magic show on the American stage. After eight years of globe-trotting, he reached London, where he bought some new and unusual illusions, among them an automatic figure of human size, called Psycho, which played a game of whist with persons from the audience.

John Nevil Maskelyne, the inventor of Psycho, had exhibited the figure in his London magical theater, known as Egyptian Hall. So when he returned to America, Kellar established his own Egyptian Hall in Philadelphia. He opened on December 15, 1884, and played for nearly a full year, featuring Psycho. His big hit, however, was his "spook cabinet." One night, Kellar induced John L. Sullivan, then the world's heavyweight champion, to sit with him in its musty gloom. Soon, John L. came bolting out with his coat gone and his vest turned inside out, taking wild punches at invisible spirits, much to the amusement of the audience.

Later, Kellar set out to challenge Herrmann, America's ruling monarch of magic, by playing opposition houses. This rivalry continued over a period of ten years, and while Herrmann's mastery still held his public, Kellar's tours proved profitable, too. The two upheld what was then America's greatest slogan: "Competition is the life of trade." Their sharp contrast in style and appearance, as well as the striking difference in the tricks and illusions that they presented, drew audiences to see both.

Truly, that was a golden era of magic, when two such masters—each classed as the "greatest magician of all time" by enthusiastic supporters—could both be seen on the American stage. Season after season, each rival added new and startling effects to his program in an effort to outshine the other. But with Herrmann's sudden death in December, 1896, the competition came to an end, and soon Kellar's sorcery was acknowledged as supreme.

During his career, Kellar's personality underwent as many changes as his magic. As he grew older, he adopted a certain austerity and grew a large, bushy mustache giving him a professorial appearance reminiscent of the Fakir of Ava. Then, one day, his mustache was gone, and later a curious tale was related regarding it.

Dramatic critics had been chiding Kellar for his poor enunciation, so he asked a well-known actor to listen from the back of the house and tell him how his voice sounded. After the show, the actor gave his frank opinion, reporting that he could hardly understand a word the magician said. At that, Kellar turned purple with rage. Rather than lose his friendship, the actor ad-libbed a wild explanation.

He blamed it all on Kellar's mustache, saying that it must have muffled his speech so that it wouldn't carry. Something like ventriloquism in reverse, was the way the actor put it. He was so earnest that Kellar took him seriously and shaved off his mustache. However, he also gave attention to his elocution, and a marked improvement followed. Also, without

93

the mustache, Kellar adopted a more natural manner, which changed his style of speech as well as his line of patter.

Kellar became the cryptic, kindly, bald-headed gentleman who looked as though he wouldn't deceive his audience for the world, and then proceeded to do exactly that. Very possibly, Kellar was the inspiration for the Wizard of Oz, for he looked the part, and L. Frank Baum wrote the first *Oz* book in 1900, when Kellar's name and face were known throughout the United States. Moreover, Kellar presented his spook act with the same air of "humbug" that characterized the fictional Wizard of Oz.

In the latter portion of his career, Kellar made a special feature of his "Rope Tie," allowing his hands to be bound behind him, then openly tapping a committeeman on the shoulder. An instant later, Kellar would turn around to show the audience that his wrists were still tied. This was done with such deft speed that Kellar seemed to have materialized a third hand for the stunt, but all the while he affected a sly innocence, as though he had nothing whatever to do with the uncanny occurrence. Actually, he had learned to slip in and out of rope ties faster than his tutors, the Davenport Brothers.

Even more weird, yet equally humorous, was Kellar's development of the "Spirit Cabinet." He used one similar to the Davenport cabinet, but with only two doors. It was put together on the stage in front of the audience, and manifestations occurred of their own accord, bells, tambourines and the like being flung from curtained holes in the doors. Spirit hands emerged and slapped Kellar's bald head, and volunteers who dared enter that dread domain were roughed up by the prankish spooks in their usual style.

The act depended on a concealed assistant, who came up through a trap in back of the cabinet while it was being assembled, then made his exit by the same route while other assistants were taking the cabinet apart.

The "Coffee and Milk" was one of Kellar's favorite tricks,

for it was admirably suited to his style. He showed two large nickel-plated containers, much like regulation cocktail shakers, which were then coming into vogue. He rattled a wand inside each shaker as he turned its mouth toward the audience, proving conclusively that the shakers were empty.

In his methodical way, Kellar then dipped his hand into a box containing brown paper shavings, bringing out some and letting them flutter back into the box. After that, he filled one shaker with brown shavings and set it on a side table. He filled the second empty shaker with white shavings from another box and set it on a similar stand.

Next, he exhibited a square of colored velvet, front and back, draping it carefully over one shaker, and taking pains to keep a portion of the shaker constantly in sight. He draped another velvet square over the second shaker in the same precise way. All was then ready for Kellar's magic. Whisking away the cloths, he poured steaming coffee from one shaker into cups that an assistant brought forward on a tray. From the other shaker he poured enough milk to fill a pitcher. This was added to the coffee, which was served to members of the audience, who were still wondering what had become of the paper shavings.

The trick depended on the boxes containing the paper shavings. Though quite ordinary, the boxes were so large that each held a hidden shaker, standing upright at one end of the box, which was turned with its broad side toward the audience. These hidden shakers were filled with coffee and milk, respectively, and each shaker was topped by a shallow metal tray, heaped with paper shavings.

In showing the empty shakers, Kellar dipped each one into a box, scooped up some shavings, poured them back, and then, to speed the process, pretended to scoop up a full shaker load all at once. Actually, he dropped the shaker and brought out the duplicate instead. This was done in one continuous action, so natural and well-rehearsed that the loaded shakers were accepted as the originals, especially since the audience had no idea that any others were involved.

Kellar added a further touch by brushing away some loose shavings from the heap, the rest being glued to the secret tray that fitted the rim of the shaker. When he covered the shakers with the velvet squares, the trick was as good as done. Through each cloth, he gripped a metal tab projecting from the tray. In removing the cloth, he carried away the tray with its shavings and dropped it on a shallow shelf, or *servante*.

All that remained was to pour coffee and milk from the shakers, clear to the last drop, showing the shakers quite as empty at the finish as they were at the start. That was the charm of Kellar's magic; where people looked for trickery, there wasn't any. The fact that the original shakers were switched for another pair was a complete throwoff.

The "Coffee and Milk" eventually became one of the most copied tricks in magic. The "original" Kellar method was listed at $5.00 in magical catalogs, while an "improved" version sold for $6.50. The "improvement" consisted of metal covers instead of the velvet squares. When placed on the shakers, the covers picked up the little trays automatically. The covers were simply laid aside, and coffee and milk were then poured from the shakers.

How the covers improved on Kellar's mastery was a mystery in itself. His handling of the velvet squares kept people watching for trickery until the final moment, whereas the metal covers made the result more mechanical. Eventually, magical dealers began selling miniature sets for as low as $2.50, so that the "Coffee and Milk" was performed by many parlor magicians.

Kellar also presented a baffling "Wine and Water" mystery. He started with a glass pitcher filled with water and a dozen empty glasses. As he poured water into the glasses, the liquid in every other glass instantly became wine. The contents were poured back into the pitcher, from which Kellar again filled the glasses, this time all with wine, except for one lone glass of water. When all were poured back into the pitcher, the contents became water. Then only wine was poured, and finally only water.

The trick depended upon chemicals, but was puzzling even to persons who suspected it, because Kellar switched in extra glasses during the pouring process. Two of these extra glasses contained a powerful bleaching agent, which Kellar concealed by cupping his hand about each glass as he presumably poured water from the pitcher. This accounted for the later transformation of wine to water, while the secret introduction of the other specially prepared glasses provided the counteracting effect of water to wine.

Many people regarded Kellar's "Flower Growth" as his masterpiece. With it, he used four tables: two, at the front of the stage, near the footlights, were undraped; the other pair, set well back, had ornamental drapes almost to the floor, but they were in keeping with the stage setting, so they roused no suspicion. On each of the ornamental rear tables was a flowerpot partly filled with earth.

In addition, Kellar had a tall, empty cone, which was open at the top to leave no doubt that it was unprepared. He entered from the left side of the stage and strode to the footlights, where he dropped a wand through the cone and showed it to be absolutely empty. Kellar then walked back to the rear table at the right and exhibited the flowerpot that was resting there. He brought a small seed from his vest pocket and planted it in the pot, which he covered with the empty cone. He raised the cone with his right hand and showed a small sprout that had apparently grown in the pot. Lifting the pot to exhibit the sprout fully, he walked forward to the undraped table at the right, set the pot there, and went back to the draped table at the rear left.

There, Kellar immediately covered the second flowerpot with

the cone and lifted it a moment later. The audience gasped at sight of a full-sized rosebush, apparently produced from nowhere; and as they did, Kellar strode forward to the undraped table at the right front, covered the pot containing the small sprout, and lifted the cone again. There, another large rosebush flowered on an undraped table.

While the audience stared dumfounded, Kellar went back to the rear left, picked up the pot and rosebush from the draped table and came forward to set them on the undraped table at the left. Curtains closed in behind Kellar, and he clipped real roses from both bushes, handing them to assistants who distributed the flowers among the audience.

Now to analyze this mystery. Behind each of the deep-draped tables at the rear was a special inner cone containing a rosebush. After showing the empty cone at the footlights, Kellar went to the rear right table, and as he brought a seed from his pocket, he palmed a small sprout and held it inside the upper end of the cone, which he placed over the pot, dropping the sprout.

As Kellar raised the cone with his right hand, he lifted the pot with his left to show the sprout. His right hand meanwhile carried the cone down in back of the draped table, picking up the hidden inner cone. He brought the pot forward to the front right table and left it there. Then he went to the rear table at the left, showed the second pot, and covered it with the cone.

A moment later, he lifted the cone, to show a full-sized rosebush, while he again carried the cone down behind the table and picked up another load. He came forward to the right and covered the pot that had the sprout. Another lift of the cone, and he had produced a second full-fledged bush. The sprout was gone from sight, behind the lower branches of the bush. Kellar then stepped back, brought the first rosebush forward and set it on the undraped table at the left. Curtains closed in behind him, hiding the long draped tables, which were forgotten by the time he and his assistant were clipping roses for the audience.

Again, Kellar's artistry was apparent. At one moment, he would be a step ahead of the audience; at another moment, he would delay his action to allay suspicion, as by picking up a load from a rear table and making his production at the front. Other magicians who watched Kellar's show often admitted that he baffled them over and over again with the "Flower Growth," so perfect was his skill in diverting attention at a crucial moment.

The "Flower Growth" was extensively copied by lesser magicians and became a stock item at magic stores. Many who bought the trick ruined it by using only the two draped tables and putting them up front because they were showy. When a bush was produced directly on each draped table, it was painfully obvious where they came from. Eventually, such tables were totally discarded, other methods being devised for concealing flower productions. But if Kellar could return tomorrow, he would still fool the wisest audience with his original routine, so deceptive was its concept.

A saying was attributed to Kellar, which ran in effect: "Once I can gain the full attention of an audience, and hold it, a brass band playing at full blast can march openly across the stage behind me, followed by a herd of elephants, yet no one will realize that they went by."

Whether or not Kellar made that extravagant claim, he lived up to it to a marked degree. He advised young magicians to improve their methods by continually learning new sleights and combining old tricks to give them a novel effect. He spun an aura of fantasy about everything he did, so that his audiences constantly expected something mysterious to happen. He watched the audience reactions and timed his great surprises to the moments when people were completely in the grip of his mystic spell.

Kellar's impact upon later generations of magicians was very pronounced, for during his heyday in the early 1900s, his competitors rapidly discarded the Mephistophelean make-up and *misterioso* manner that had characterized the Herrmann era. But merely adopting Kellar's cryptic expression and occasionally whimsical style was not the answer.

It took inborn craft to captivate an audience, and Kellar had that gift. This was evidenced by the fact that he presented his large illusions with the same éclat he displayed with the smaller feats of legerdemain, which had won him his great fame. Here, again, Kellar was a perfectionist, depending upon a few fine illusions rather than an overwhelming array.

Greatest of these was the "Levitation of Princess Karnac." A girl in Hindu costume was hypnotized and placed upon a couch in the center of the fully lighted stage. She then floated slowly upward until she was suspended six feet in air. The couch was removed and Kellar ascended a short step-ladder from which he passed a solid hoop completely about the floating lady. The couch was replaced, the girl floated downward in the same mysterious fashion and was awakened from her trance.

The noted magical author, John Northern Hilliard, wrote the following description of the "levitation scene" that appeared in Kellar's program:

> The most daring and bewildering illusion and by far the most difficult achievement Mr. Kellar ever attempted. Absolutely new in principle. The dream in midair of the dainty Princess of Karnac surpasses the fabled feats of the ancient Egyptian sorcerers, nor can anything more magical be found in the pages of the Thousand and One Nights, and it lends a resemblance to the miraculous tales of levitation that come out of India.
>
> This illusion is acknowledged by critics and historians of the goetic art to be the profoundest achievement in either ancient or modern magic. Its perfection represents fifteen years of patient research and abstruse study, and the ex-

penditure of as many thousands of dollars. The result of these labors is a veritable masterpiece of magic, the sensational marvel of the twentieth century and the crowning achievement of Mr. Kellar's long and brilliant career.

The levitation principle probably did originate in India, for in 1832 a fakir named Sheshal astounded the citizenry of Madras by placing one hand upon an upright staff set in a small platform and squatting comfortably in mid-air with no other support. This was accomplished by means of a hidden rod extending from the staff into the fakir's sleeve, then down his back to form a semicircular seat.

The "Aerial Suspension" later performed by Robert-Houdin, Anderson and others, was an outgrowth of that Hindu trick, but the fact that the person reclined straight outward, with only an elbow resting on the pole, was a great improvement. However, the ultimate aim of every modern magician was to float a person in mid-air with no visible support whatever.

That was achieved in the 1870s by John Nevil Maskelyne, at Egyptian Hall in London. A framework equipped with block and tackle stood behind the rear curtain of the small stage. From the frame, a horizontal rod extended through a slit in the curtain to a skeleton cradle hidden in the cushions of a couch.

The magician pretended to hypnotize an assistant, who was placed upon the couch. A stagehand operated the device behind the curtain, causing the person to rise with the unseen cradle and descend slowly to the couch. Later, wires were used instead of the block and tackle, so that the illusion could be presented well forward on the stage, and this was the version that Kellar developed into the "Levitation of Princess Karnac."

Kellar used two sets of wires that were so thin they blended with the pattern of the backdrop and could not be seen. One set ran upward from the center of a short bar that extended back from the cradle on which the girl lay. These wires went

101

to a gridiron high in the scenery. There, a cable continued to a winch offstage, and when this was turned, the girl would rise and descend as required.

The other set of wires ran downward from the back end of the bar through holes in the stage to weights that hung beneath. The weights counterbalanced the girl's body and prevented the cradle from tipping forward while the levitation was in progress.

The effect of a Hindu princess floating unsupported in the center of a lighted stage was incredible enough, but the passing of the hoop around the girl's body left the onlookers utterly bewildered. Kellar worked the hoop-passing by means of "gooseneck" between the cradle and the wires. That portion of the bar was S-shaped, which enable him to draw the hoop from the girl's feet almost to her head, the rear portion of the hoop entering one bend of the S. He then swung the front portion around the girl's head and thrust the hoop toward her feet, behind her body.

During that thrust, each side of the hoop followed a different slot in the S bar, and at the finish, Kellar simply swung the far end around the girl's feet. He then drew the hoop from feet to head again, bringing it clear and handing it to an assistant, who carried it into the audience for examination. Apparently, Kellar had passed the hoop completely around the girl twice, a most convincing procedure and quite unfathomable to anyone who had never heard of a gooseneck or an S bar.

Kellar's full evening show consisted of three acts. In 1904 he engaged Paul Valadon, an accomplished sleight-of-hand artist, to present the second part. Valadon had worked at Egyptian Hall in London, and had helped Kellar construct the improved levitation, so he was well versed in the presentation of stage illusions as well as sleights.

Valadon was slated to become Kellar's successor, but they parted company after a few seasons and Howard Thurston joined Kellar in Valadon's place. The Fakir of Ava had retired comfortably at the age of sixty and had lived another twenty years, so perhaps Kellar felt that sixty might be his magic number too. He was in his sixtieth year when he bestowed his wizard's mantle upon Thurston at Ford's Opera House in Baltimore on May 9, 1908.

That date stands as the most dramatic in the annals of modern magic, for on no other occasion has an acknowledged master of the craft publicly turned over his wand to a successor. As Kellar and Thurston shook hands in front of the final curtain, the orchestra played "Auld Lang Syne" and the entire audience arose and joined in the chorus, while teams of ushers brought up huge floral offerings from Kellar's friends. There were tears in Kellar's eyes as he viewed a stage flooded with bouquets of roses that for the first time were not the product of his own mysterious skill.

After Kellar retired, he built a home in southern California and constructed a miniature theater where he tried out new magical effects, including an improved levitation. Often, he had the urge to return to the road, but only once did he come from retirement. That was during World War I, when he headlined a benefit performance given by magicians at the New York Hippodrome.

By then, Kellar was considered the dean of magic, and many of his fellow wizards felt that "Kellar Day," as they termed the event, should be celebrated annually. Curiously, the wish was prophetic, for the date happened to be November 11, 1917. Exactly one year later, the Armistice was signed, ending World War I, so Kellar Day has fallen on a holiday ever since.

Following that final public appearance, Kellar continued to give private performances in his little theater almost until his last brief illness, which ended in his death on March 10, 1922.

Chapter 5

CHUNG LING SOO

(1861–1918)

When Billy Robinson was not quite twenty years of age, he called himself the "Man of Mystery" and appeared as a magician in his own show, with a company of assistants. That was in 1880, when railroads were spreading throughout the country and already formed a close network in New England, where the "Man of Mystery" gave most of his performances.

It was easy to reach small but thriving industrial towns, hire a hall, put on an evening's show and then go on by train the next day. Sometimes the troupe would travel by stagecoach, using horses and wagons to haul the equipment over back roads to towns on other railroad lines. From such small beginnings, young Robinson hoped some day to become the world's greatest magician and travel not only throughout the United States, but abroad as well, for he was sure he had a show that represented the magic of the future.

Of course, the youthful "Man of Mystery" presented many of the popular tricks of the day; no magic show would have been complete without them. He vanished playing cards and caused them to reappear at the points of a large metal star. He mixed wine and water in a decanter and made the liquids separate, arriving mysteriously in different glasses. He caught coins from the air and tossed them into a high hat that he had borrowed from the audience. Then, as a climax, he produced from the hat all sorts of articles, ranging from vegetables and bird cages to heavy cannon balls. But his show did not end with that.

While still a schoolboy in New York, Billy had seen or heard of many noted magicians, like the venerable Signor Blitz, with his marvelous automatic devices; and Wyman the Wizard, who featured a "gift show" in which every member of the audience received a prize. He had also seen the performances of Robert Heller, the first magician to introduce a mind-reading act on the American stage; and he had witnessed the ghostly demonstrations of the Davenport Brothers.

Intrigued by all this, Billy had read every book on magic that he could find. After finishing school, he had taken up the trade of metalworker, so that he was able to construct magical equipment, of his own. With this equipment, he performed mind-reading feats like Heller, and outdid the spooky tricks of the Davenports, using similar effects of his own invention. As magician, mind reader and medium, Robinson was truly a "Man of Mystery," giving his audiences three acts for the price of one. But he found that it was too much for them to appreciate all at once.

After a few unsuccessful seasons, Robinson joined a variety show in Boston and began doing a shorter act. The show toured the larger New England cities where the audiences, too, were larger and more appreciative of his skill. On one tour, he met and later married a dancer named Olive Path, who was nicknamed "Dot" because she was so small. Soon, Dot was assisting Billy in his magic act and they were saving toward a big show of their own.

A break came in 1887 when Robinson heard of a new type of magic called "Black Art" which had been popularized in Europe by a performer named Max Auzinger, who called himself Ben Ali Bey and appeared in Oriental costume. Another illusionist, Buatier de Kolta, was planning a similar act at Egyptian Hall in London. From descriptions, Robinson recognized that the "Black Art" act must depend on special lighting equipment far superior to the flickery gas footlights of the average New England variety hall.

Robinson also knew that two enterprising theater men, B. F. Keith and E. F. Albee, were planning America's first important vaudeville circuit. They had already opened the Bijou Theatre in Boston and the new Gaiety in Providence. Both houses had all the latest stage equipment, so Robinson approached Keith and Albee. As he hoped, they were looking for unusual attractions. They billed Robinson under the name of Achmed Ben Ali, and he put on the "Black Art" act for nearly seven months much in the style of the original Ben Ali Bey.

And what an act it was!

Beyond the brilliant footlights and bright lights at the sides, the audience saw a barren stage, looming like a huge black cavern. Robinson made his entrance dressed in white robes and turban, and sporting a flowing white beard. With a wave of his hand, he plucked a white wand from nowhere. He waved the wand and a tall table, shaped like a pedestal, appeared instantly upon the stage.

The magician rapped the table to prove it solid and produced another table in the same mysterious style, this one on the other side of the stage. Two waves of the wand and a large wooden vase appeared upon one table; then a second vase appeared on the other. The white-robed wizard picked up the first vase and thumped it upon the table to prove it solid. By then, the amazed audience was staring at the other side of the stage because the second vase was going through the same gyrations, without the aid of a human hand!

Uncannily, the vase remained floating in mid-air. The magician picked up a white hoop, walked over and passed the hoop all around the vase, to prove that it was unsupported. Then the vase descended slowly, gracefully to the table, landing with a defiant thump.

More marvels followed in rapid succession: White tennis balls materialized from nowhere, as did white rabbits; when the wizard tossed them in air, they vanished. A skeleton made a fantastic appearance, limb by limb; its legs, arms, ribs and skull turned somersaults in air and finally assembled themselves, only to disappear at the magician's command.

For a finish, the magician picked up a white sheet and wrapped himself inside it, mummy fashion. Gradually, the sheet unwound itself and fell crumpled to the stage. The magician was gone! But a moment later he reappeared, robe, beard and all, dashing down the aisle and up onto the stage to take a final bow.

Amazing though the act was, the method was not complicated. The entire stage—sides, back, ceiling, even the floor—was covered with black velvet. The brilliant gas burners, at the front, were equipped with reflectors, throwing the glare away from the stage and directly toward the audience. That made the blackness solid and impenetrable. Anything covered with black velvet or hidden behind a cloth of that material, was totally invisible. Only white objects could be seen.

At the start of the act, the tables, vases and other objects were concealed beneath black velvet covers that could be zipped away in an instant. When Robinson walked on in the white regalia of Achmed Ben Ali, little Dot was standing by, completely clad in black velvet, with hood and gloves, which enabled her to walk anywhere about the stage, totally unseen.

When Achmed Ben Ali reached into the air, his invisible assistant whipped a white wand from the folds of her black costume and let him pluck it from space. As he waved the wand toward one side of the stage, Dot yanked away the cover from one table, then skipped across the stage to do the same with the table on the other side. The vases were similarly unveiled at the wizard's command. While Robinson was thumping one vase on the table, Dot did the same with the other, giving the effect that it was acting on its own.

The passing of the white hoop about the floating vase was

a bit more difficult. Dot held the vase with her right hand at the back edge of the rim and down inside, so her black glove would not show against the white. As Robinson passed the hoop slowly up over the vase, Dot slid her left hand beneath, setting the vase on it. By the time the hoop reached the top of the vase, Dot was able to draw her right hand away, so that the hoop could clear.

Tennis balls and rabbits were brought from under cover by Dot and handed to Robinson as he reached for them. When the wizard tossed them in the air, his unseen assistant caught them in a black velvet bag, which hid the objects completely. The skeleton, painted in white on a black board, had removable sections, so its limbs and skull could gyrate independently. To vanish it, the assistant threw a black cloth over the upright board.

The finale was clever indeed. The white sheet that Robinson used was backed by a black cloth. As he raised the sheet, Dot stepped in and took it from him, holding it in front of him while he wrapped himself in the black cloth. He was then able to walk offstage unseen, while his assistant began wrapping herself in the sheet.

At the proper moment, Dot let the sheet drop. Being all in black, she could not be seen; and the effect was the sudden disappearance of the wizard, who was supposedly still in the sheet. Meanwhile Robinson had gotten rid of his own black cloth and had hurried from the stage door around to the auditorium. He then dashed up on to the stage, where he picked up and displayed the empty sheet from which he had seemingly vanished only a few seconds before.

The Robinsons, or more correctly, Achmed Ben Ali and Company, added new effects weekly to their "Black Art" act. With the aid of a second assistant, also clad in black, they sped up the transposition of objects; and the mysterious Achmed Ben Ali later produced a white frame containing a living "Half

Lady" who was visible only from the waist up, as she swung in mid-air.

The Half Lady, of course, was Dot, still wearing the lower portion of her black costume. She simply took her position behind a white-painted swing, from which the other assistant whisked away a black cloth at Robinson's cue.

Oddly, the very success of the "Black Art" act was Robinson's undoing. Many magicians came to see the new sensation, among them Herrmann the Great and his principal rival, Harry Kellar. Each wanted to buy the "Black Art" act and Kellar asked the Robinsons to travel along with his show and work in it as well. Billy was still young, only about twenty-six years of age, and to him this seemed a great opportunity, so he put aside his own ambitions and went with Kellar.

In theaters that had the right equipment, Robinson worked the "Black Art" act as part of the Kellar show, calling himself Nana Sahib, with Dot and members of the Kellar troupe as his assistants. He also developed new and remarkable illusions for Kellar. In the one called "Astarte," Dot appeared as a white-clad maiden who floated gracefully in mid-air at Kellar's command, turning somersaults high above the stage. This involved "black art" on a modified scale, the support being a long, specially-geared metal rod covered with velvet and extending from a black backdrop against which it was unseen.

In 1893, after five years with Kellar, the Robinsons received a better offer from Herrmann and switched to his show. Again, Billy performed the "Black Art" as a special act, now working under the name of Abdul Khan; and Dot appeared in an improved form of the "Astarte" illusion, as Florine, "Child of the Air." With Herrmann, the peerless prestidigitator, facing the audience, and Robinson, the master mechanician, behind the scenes, the art of modern magic was nearing the peak of perfection.

But when Alexander Herrmann suddenly died in 1896, the

whole picture changed. Leon Herrmann tried to fill the master magician's place and Robinson stayed with the show for three years, helping him carry on. Then Leon switched to vaudeville, where he managed to gain good engagements on the strength of the Herrmann name.

Robinson, too, returned to vaudeville, once more as the "Man of Mystery." Dot worked the "Astarte" act under the title of the "Maid in the Moon" in the glow of a huge spotlight, for by now electric lights had supplanted gaslights in most theaters. But the act, though suited to the new and palatial vaudeville houses that had replaced the old variety halls, was too tame for the more exacting audiences, who demanded novelty.

That was provided in May, 1899, when a totally unheard-of wizard arrived in New York and took the vaudeville world by storm. The newcomer was Ching Ling Foo, a Chinese magician brought to America by some enterprising promoters.

Attired in a large, flowing silk robe, Ching Ling Foo waddled onto the stage, exhibited a Chinese silk cloth back and front, gave it a forward fling and slowly raised it to reveal a large china bowl, a foot and a half high, and the same in diameter. Amazingly, the bowl was filled with water, as was proven by a dozen apples bobbing on its surface. The water was poured out, filling three buckets and weighing nearly one hundred pounds, bowl included.

After following with a few Chinese tricks done in slow, bland style, Ching Ling Foo bowed off to great applause from the audience, which still wondered where the huge bowl had come from. Then the Chinese wizard waddled on again, gave the cloth another fling, and from it produced a Chinese boy, who took a bow along with the magician.

To conclude his act, Ching Ling Foo showed a bowl of bran, took heaping spoonfuls from it and stuffed them into his mouth. Suddenly, he blew out smoke, followed by great jets of flame and explosive bursts that left the audience astounded as the curtain fell. By then, the spectators felt there was only one answer to the wonders of Ching Ling Foo. They were magic, because they could be nothing else.

But they weren't magic to Billy Robinson, who went to see the act for himself. Later, at home in a little bookshop that he had opened on East Eighty-eighth Street, Billy described the trick to Dot, and drew sketches showing exactly how the bowl production worked.

It depended on a special harness worn by the Chinese wizard, with a hanging cord and self-releasing hook from which the bowl was suspended behind his legs, hidden by the skirt of his robe. This accounted for his waddly walk. To produce the bowl, he simply flung the cloth forward, spread his legs so the bowl contacted the stage, and stepped back. The hook released automatically when the bowl touched the stage; the water couldn't spill out because the bowl was covered with a special sheet of waterproof material that Ching Ling Foo took away with the cloth. As for the boy who appeared from beneath the cloth later, he simply walked in with his legs behind the magician's and his body and head under the back of the robe. When the cloth was flung out, the boy came forward and appeared beneath it.

Billy didn't have to explain the fire act to Dot. They had both seen fire-eaters in the dime museums where they had worked their own act in the early days when vaudeville dates were few. In pretending to swallow wads of cotton, a fire-eater would pick up a few containing bits of smoldering punk, the sort used for setting off fireworks.

By holding these between his teeth, the fire-eater could exhale his breath and send out showers of sparks and clouds of smoke. The old wads were secretly removed when the performer stuffed new quantities of cotton into his mouth. In these were strips of chemically treated paper that ignited when the fire-eater again exhaled, spurting flames like a human volcano.

The Chinese were noted for their fireworks and Ching Ling Foo had brought some pyrotechnic tidbits from his native land.

When he ladled bran into his mouth, he introduced tiny coils of tightly rolled paper that he disgorged in the form of colored streamers. In these were tiny firecrackers and fireballs that exploded when blown outward, forming a fantastic finale.

To Robinson it was tame compared to some of the dime museum fire-eating acts, and what amazed him most was how the public could be impressed by such old tricks. Still, Ching Ling Foo was getting vaudeville engagements and Robinson wasn't. When the Chinese wizard was held over for an extended engagement at Keith's Theatre, the management offered a reward to anyone who could duplicate the famous bowl trick. So Robinson bought a Chinese robe and a bowl bigger than Foo's with a tight-fitting rubber cover and constructed a harness of his own invention. He packed the outfit in a big suitcase and took it to the theater where Ching Ling Foo was appearing, but the offer was immediately withdrawn.

From New York, Ching Ling Foo toured the United States, creating a sensation in every vaudeville theater where he appeared. Local magicians copied his act, but with little success, for the novelty soon wore off and nobody came up with anything new to match the giant fish bowl. Meanwhile, Billy Robinson was tending his bookshop in New York and filling occasional engagements as the "Man of Mystery." When those dates dwindled, Billy went to see a theatrical agent named Ike Rose, who booked acts in England, where magic was highly popular. But Rose doubted that he could sell Robinson there.

Several American magicians had scored a great success in England because their acts were unique. There was Downs, who had turned the old coin-catching act into a real sensation. Calling himself the "King of Koins," he plucked hundreds of half-dollars from the glare of spotlights. There was Thurston, the amazing card manipulator. There was Houdini, the man whom neither handcuffs nor jails could hold. So when Robinson talked of vanishing doves from cages and producing girls from empty cabinets, he did not strike the modern note that the public wanted.

Still, Robinson's list of illusions was impressive. He had created the "Escape from Sing Sing" and the "Mid-air Vanish," along with "Vanity Fair" and the "Palanquin Production." Ike Rose decided that those and other of Robinson's creations might make feature attractions at the Folies Bergère, the leading vaudeville theater in France. Ike cabled Paris and arranged an extended engagement on that basis. Within a few weeks, the Robinsons were on a steamship bound for France, accompanied by their new manager.

Included in their baggage were the Hindu costumes and velvet curtains for the "Black Art" act and the Chinese robe and bowl that Robinson had bought when he challenged Ching Ling Foo. Ike Rose had insisted upon bringing those props along, because with them, Robinson could change his personality as well as his act. After stressing this point, Ike added that when they finally reached England, Robinson could do a big show his own way.

Billy smiled when he heard that, but his smile was grim and it worried Dot. She realized that in those years with Kellar and Herrmann, Robinson had lost his old enthusiasm through watching others play the part of the magician while he was relegated to stage manager. He did his old routines well enough before an average audience, but his style had become methodical and impassive.

Dot dreaded the opening night at the Folies Bergère, and when the time arrived, on April 15, 1900, her worst fears were realized. Unlike American vaudeville, where each performer was on his own, the show at the Folies Bergère was a lively, exciting revue, in which each act caught the gaiety and carried on in the same tempo, to the increasing enthusiasm of the audience.

As the show picked up momentum, Robinson made his preparations in his own meticulous way, paying no heed to anything else. When the curtain rose, he walked onstage and bowed stiffly, as though about to make an announcement to a serious audience. The gay crowd mistook his manner for comedy and a ripple of laughter emerged from the hollow darkness of the auditorium, the first that had ever greeted Robinson at the opening of his act. It disconcerted him.

Back in America, Robinson could have met the situation with a few clever opening remarks; but here in Paris, he could only force a smile and give an awkward shrug. With that, he lost all the dignity of the magician and the audience was convinced that this must be a comedy act. It soon became one, but unintentionally. Robinson started his first trick, only to find that his assistants were not ready, so he made another apologetic bow that brought roars of laughter. Robinson bungled one trick, then the next, and the assistants missed more cues. The laughter turned to hisses as the audience realized that this was not comedy, but simply a fiasco. Still a showman, Robinson tried to address the audience with what little French he could command, but by then, the signal had been given to lower the curtain.

A dejected, bewildered figure, Robinson found himself facing an angry manager, who was shouting in French that Billy could understand, even without knowing the full meaning of the words. He gathered that his act was no good and that it was an insult to the audience. At that point, Ike Rose arrived to intervene. He mollified the manager and assured him that Robinson would put on a different act—and a better one—the next night.

One thing was certain, Billy couldn't appear again as Robinson, or he would be laughed off the stage. But Ike Rose had an answer for that. He told Billy to put on his Chinese robe and work a few Oriental tricks, finishing with the production of the big bowl. Instead of Robinson, the Man of Mystery, he would be Hop Sing Loo, the Chinese wizard. As an added touch, the act would include Fee Lung, a genuine Chinese acrobat, who had come with the troupe from New York.

The next night the act went on. Wearing Chinese make-up with his robe, Robinson looked like a real Celestial wizard. Tiny Dot, also attired in Chinese costume, made a perfect assistant, and the tricks went smoothly indeed, though they were of a routine sort, with rice appearing in boxes, birds disappearing from cages, and other minor mysteries that intrigued the sophisticated spectators, but did not quite amaze them.

That very fact pleased Robinson, because he was building up to his great surprise, the bowl production. He finished his lesser routines and bowed off to a fair round of applause as Fee Lung came somersaulting on the stage, carrying lighted torches for an acrobatic fire dance. During that number, Robinson was backstage, getting set for the finale.

Time was short, for acts worked speedily at the Folies Bergère. Even with Dot's aid, Billy just had time to hook the bowl in its harness, when the cue came for him to waddle onstage. What happened then has never quite been explained. Either the bowl was not hitched properly, or Robinson put too much gusto into the bowl production as he reached the footlights and gave the cloth a spreading fling in front of him.

He produced the bowl all right. But it came swinging forward so rapidly that it hit the stage at an angle, and as Robinson stepped backward, whipping the cloth away, the bowl toppled forward and poured its entire contents down into the orchestra pit, to the wild, hysterical delight of the audience.

By the time the curtain fell, the manager was backstage shouting imprecations that made his previous night's outburst seem mild. Reduced to simple terms, it meant that Robinson was through. That was verified by Ike Rose, when he joined Billy and Dot at a little café where they had gone to mourn over their misery.

However, Ike was still optimistic. He had made the best out

115

of a bad situation by canceling the engagement at the Folies Bergère, with the understanding that the flop would be forgotten and that there would be no adverse reports. The manager of the Alhambra Theatre of London was due in Paris the next day and Ike had intended to take him to the Folies Bergère to see Robinson, the Man of Mystery. Instead, Ike would now tell him about Robinson, the great American illusionist, who would soon be arriving from New York with tons of wonderful equipment and might be induced to open in London instead of Paris.

But it did not work out quite that way. When Ike met the man from the Alhambra and began to talk about a magic act, the Londoner cut him short before he could even mention the magician's name. There were so many magic acts in England that they could be had for a shilling a dozen. Only one magician could possible interest the Alhambra. That was the sensational Chinese wizard who had toured America and returned to China without even visiting England. He would surely score a hit in London.

At that point, the Alhambra manager started to give the name of the Chinese magician. It began with "Ching Ling" or "Chung Ling," but he couldn't recall the rest. Ike knew that the Londoner meant Ching Ling Foo, but it was easy to change it further. So Ike remarked, "You must mean Chung Ling Soo." The Londoner nodded, never realizing that the name had been coined for his benefit. Then Ike blandly announced that Chung Ling Soo happened to be the very magician he was bringing to Europe, and that he would be ready to open with a completely new show in about a month.

A magician is supposed to amaze everyone, his manager included. But that day, Robinson was utterly amazed by his manager, who brought in a contract calling for him to open at the Alhambra Theatre, in London, on May 14, not as himself, but as a Chinese wizard named Chung Ling Soo, who until now had never existed.

Ike told Robinson to pick out his best and biggest illusions and paint or rebuild them in Chinese style. Where he had tables, he was to use taborets. All the costumes and scenery were to be Chinese, the more splendid the better. It was to be the big act that Robinson had hoped to do in London, but with an Oriental setting, and above all, he was never to forget that he was Chung Ling Soo.

Billy Robinson never did forget it.

During the next month, he lived and dreamed the part of Chung Ling Soo. With Dot, now known as Suee Seen, or "Water Lily," he rehearsed each trick as rapidly as the apparatus was converted to Chinese form. For costumes, Billy and Dot chose the most lavish that they could find in the Chinese shops of London's Limehouse district.

The Soo show overwhelmed a capacity audience on the opening night at the London Alhambra. Attired in the crimson regalia of a Chinese mandarin, Chung Ling Soo instantly produced two doves from between plates of bran; and then proceeded to extract huge, garish silken streamers from a row of empty tubes. Next, the mandarin magician introduced a sensational fire-eating act. He bowed off to tremendous applause while Fee Lung did an acrobatic act, swinging from a trapeze by his pigtail. When Chung Ling Soo returned for his final bow, he produced the big bowl at the footlights, this time in perfect style.

Never before had London theatergoers seen such magic, though it must be conceded that they had never witnessed a performance by the genuine Chinese wizard, Ching Ling Foo, who had turned down offers to come to England. At the same time, to the credit of the self-styled Chung Ling Soo, he was no mere imitator, but a master showman in his own right, who had adopted Chinese guise because it was the vogue and also because it enabled him to perform his own version of the giant bowl production.

Actually, the bowl trick was a very old one, worked by many

magicians in China (Ching Ling Foo just happened to be the first to show it outside of his native land), so Robinson felt free to introduce it in England while performing under the name of Chung Ling Soo. In any case, he rapidly followed up his sudden success by introducing new effects that created even more of a sensation than the giant bowl production.

One of the first of these was the "Aerial Fishing" mystery, which Chung Ling Soo advertised as a feat of Chinese wizardry, though it was actually of American origin. From Suee Seen, Chung Ling Soo took a long fishing rod with a line and a hook on the end. To the hook, he affixed a tiny bit of bait, which appeared to be about a half-inch portion of a worm. Gazing intently into the air, he extended the end of the pole over the footlights so that the baited hook dangled above the heads of the audience, as he swept it back and forth. Then he whipped the pole upward.

Instantly, a squirming goldfish appeared upon the hook, glittering in the spotlight, struggling to get away as Soo swung the end of the line toward himself. The Chinese wizard deftly plucked the goldfish from the hook and dropped it into a glass bowl of water held by Suee Seen. There, the fish swam about excitedly while the magician again baited his hook and made another cast above the heads of the audience. Again, he caught a shimmering goldfish on the hook and tossed it into the bowl with the first. Again and again, he swung the line with its baited hook, catching a third goldfish, a fourth, a fifth—all alive and wriggling—until the bowl appeared to be a mass of gold.

That one trick brought thousands of people to see Chung Ling Soo. They watched the sleeves of his mandarin robe, as well as Suee Seen's, thinking the fish might come from there; but the fish were always a dozen feet or more beyond the magician's reach when they materialized on the hook. The closer people looked, the more nonplussed they became.

The trick lay partly in the bits of bait which Chung Ling

Soo placed on the hook. What the audience mistook for tiny worms or small metal sinkers, were actually hollow tubes, no more than an inch in length. Inside each was a coiled strip of thin silk cloth, about the size and shape of a goldfish and appropriately colored. The "head" was attached to the tube by a silk thread, so that when the "fish" was uncoiled, the "tail" would dangle free.

When Chung Ling Soo was ready to produce a fish from mid-air, he would finish a sweep of the rod with an upward jerk, much as a fisherman would, when a real fish snapped a baited hook. The action caused the hidden coil of silk to fall from the tube and the effect was exactly as if a live fish had appeared on the end of the line. As long as the pole was kept in motion, the fluttering cloth continued to convey the illusion of a squirming fish, materialized from nowhere.

That, however, was only half the trick. The handle of the fishing rod had a row of short compartments, end to end, each of which could be opened with a sideways twist. These were lined with wet cotton and just before the trick a live fish was placed in each compartment, which was then closed.

After catching a silken "fish" the magician raised the pole and let the hook swing toward him, at the same time releasing a fish from the handle of the rod into his hand. Holding the rod in his other hand, he reached up, took the silken fish, tube and all, and dropped it into the bowl with the live goldfish. The metal tube sank to the bottom with the silken fake, so that the audience saw only the live fish swimming about.

The switch was so natural, yet so artful, that Chung Ling Soo repeated it time after time in the same bland, deceptive manner, without fear of detection.

This was but one of many baffling novelties that Billy Robinson introduced into the act that he now performed with utter perfection in the guise of Chung Ling Soo. Actually, he had begun to live the part of a Chinese wizard, and that was the real secret of his remarkable success as he toured England and returned to London more famous than ever.

Offstage as well as on, Billy wore the Chinese costume and make-up of Chung Ling Soo, while Dot played the part of Suee Seen. Wherever they went, they attracted crowds, and Chung Ling Soo bowed to the plaudits of admirers with a cryptic smile that seemed authentically Chinese. Well did he remember how the Great Herrmann had gained attention with his pointed mustache and goatee. Herrmann's satanic appearance had impressed the American public; now, his one-time assistant was capturing the fancy of the British populace in a similar but even craftier style.

Fee Lung and other members of the company were genuine Chinese, which helped the pretense. They were sworn to secrecy regarding the true identity of Chung Ling Soo, and, indeed, they played a part in the game. When newspapermen wanted to interview Chung Ling Soo, they were informed by Ike Rose that the mandarin magician, with all his skill and wisdom, could not speak a single word of English. It was against the scruples of those close to the court of the Chinese empress dowager—as Chung Ling Soo was—to contaminate their own pure speech with a foreign tongue.

So the newsmen had to talk through an interpreter, a role fulfilled by Fee Lung. They put their questions in English and Fee Lung repeated them in Chinese. Chung Ling Soo responded in a meaningless singsong that passed as the cultured language of the dowager's court. Most of the questions were routine, and Fee Lung anwered them in his own way. However, if Chung Ling Soo heard any that he didn't want to answer, he changed the tone of his singsong as a cue for Fee Lung to ignore them.

This went on for years. In London, Chung Ling Soo lived in an apartment that was lavish with Chinese decorations. He appeared upon the street in his mandarin attire, with a Chinese attendant holding a huge Oriental umbrella above his head.

Meanwhile he added new and fabulous mysteries to his act, among them the celebrated "Bullet Catching Trick."

There were two reasons why Soo did the "Bullet Catch." The first was that it had been worked successfully and sensationally by Herrmann the Great, when Soo—as Robinson—had been his master mechanic. The trick, which involved firing a loaded gun point-blank at the magician, was foolproof the way Robinson had perfected it.

The other reason was that the trick represented an ideal device to turn a potentially serious political problem to his advantage. At the very time when Soo had become the biggest vaudeville headliner in England, there was an outburst of rabid nationalists in China, known as the Boxer Rebellion. Members of European legations were attacked and slain, missionaries were massacred, and thousands of other foreigners were threatened, until an expeditionary force composed of troops of various nations—Americans and British among them—marched to Peking, took over the Chinese capital, and restored order.

In England there was a surge of indignation against China and the Chinese in general, which put Chung Ling Soo in a real dilemma. If he continued to masquerade as a Chinese, he was likely to be hissed off the stage; if he revealed the fact that he was an American, his act would lose its glamour and he might be ridiculed as an impostor.

To preserve his pretended identity, he adopted a bold tack. He announced to the press that he was a member of a mandarin group who were friendly to foreigners. That, in fact, was why he had been forced to leave China and tour as a magician, something that no mandarin had ever done before. The story grew as Soo concocted new details and disclosed them through his interpreter. Eventually it developed that he had been captured by Boxers when their insurrection was still in its secret stage. They had condemned him to death before the firing squad, but through sheer sorcery, he had

121

rendered their bullets harmless, and thus had escaped death.

To back this incredible story, Chung Ling Soo duplicated the feat upon the stage, and it became a spectacular attraction. At the finish of one scene, Fee Lung stepped to the footlights and announced in pidgin English that Chung Ling Soo would show how he escaped death at the hands of the Boxers. He invited two gentlemen from the audience to serve as a committee and supervise the loading of the guns.

While the volunteers were coming up the steps to the stage, garish dragon curtains parted, and Chung Ling Soo, garbed as a Chinese war lord, was marched onstage by a firing squad wearing Boxer uniforms and broad-brimmed hats. To the discordant gong beats of an Oriental dirge, the victim took his place before the firing squad, while two of its members handed their old-fashioned muzzle-loading rifles to the committeemen for thorough examination.

Suee Seen, meanwhile, went down into the audience with two bullets, which spectators marked with identifying scratches from a knife point, and dropped into a cup that she carried. Suee Seen brought the bullets back to the stage and they were loaded into the muzzles of the examined guns, along with powder and paper wadding, each charge being rammed tightly home with a regulation ramrod.

Chung Ling Soo took his place at one side of the stage, holding a china plate in front of his chest, like a target. At the other side, two members of the firing squad faced him with the loaded rifles. The music stopped, the audience was hushed, as a Boxer officer barked the Chinese words for "Ready—aim—fire!"

Both guns blasted and Chung's tall figure reeled, only to rally as a great gasp of horror swept the audience. He gave the plate a sweep as he came upward; and there, rolling upon it, glittering in the spotlight, were two silvery bullets, caught from mid-air!

Striding across the stage, Chung Ling Soo let the committeemen see the charmed bullets; then, openly, he spilled them into the little cup held by Suee Seen, who went down the steps and delivered them to the amazed persons who had marked them and now identified them as the very same bullets.

Few people really believed that Chung Ling Soo had staged that act before an actual firing squad, but the trick itself baffled British audiences, and established the fact that Chung Ling Soo was anti-Boxer. The trick was something of a puzzle to magicians, too, for though they knew the general principles of the "Bullet Catch" there was something in Soo's method that they couldn't quite fathom.

A few years after the Boxer crisis, Chung Ling Soo was confronted with another problem. The real Chinese wizard, Ching Ling Foo, had lost much of his fortune after his return to China, due to the Boxer trouble. He decided to make up for it with another grand tour, this time including Europe on his route. In December, 1904, Ching Ling Foo arrived in London with a company of Chinese jugglers, contortionists and acrobats. His troupe opened as the headline attraction at the Empire Theatre.

By odd coincidence, Chung Ling Soo had just brought his show into the London Hippodrome, only a block away; and the public was treated to the sight of rival banners, proclaiming each to be the greatest Chinese wizard of all time. It was a case of "pay your money and take your choice," and a great many people did both, in order to compare the contending Chinese conjurors and their claims.

But the fad did not last long. Capacity crowds began to dwindle at the Empire, while the shows at the Hippodrome were sellouts. The reason was simply this: Ching Ling Foo was doing the same old Chinese tricks, the only ones he knew, and though he did them perfectly, they were "old hat" to the jaded London vaudeville-goers, who constantly craved novelty.

And novelty was what Chung Ling Soo gave them. His

stock in trade was the creation of new illusions, in which the most advanced notions in American and European mechanical devices were concealed within the innocent folds of Chinese dragon drapes and beneath the lacquered shells of taborets and cabinets. Ching's genuine Chinese tricks seemed outmoded, simply because Chung had performed and discarded them long before.

In desperation Ching Ling Foo challenged Chung Ling Soo to a display of skill before newsmen in the office of the London *Despatch.* The terms were: Ching would forfeit five thousand dollars if Chung could perform ten out of twenty tricks that Ching would show the committee, or if he, Ching, was unable to duplicate any trick that Chung might do.

It was a shrewd stratagem. As a manipulative magician, Ching Ling Foo was a past master. He knew dozens of close-up tricks that could baffle the sharpest eye, some of them never before seen outside of China. Indeed, it was Ching's specialty in small tricks that limited his stage presentations to a few large ones. On the other hand, Chung Ling Soo specialized in mechanical magic and wouldn't even be able to get his big equipment into the newspaper office. It seemed unlikely that Chung could come up with even one close-range effect that Ching could not follow.

There was just one flaw in Ching's logic: The former Billy Robinson was the best-read, most-informed person in the magic business; his library of magical books, at the time of its disposal, was the largest in America. Robinson had furnished explanations for many tricks and illusions to the *Scientific American;* and he had written a book on *Spirit Slate Writing,* exposing the tricks of fake mediums. In addition, he had watched the Great Herrmann perform some of the finest of close-up feats. Out of that vast storehouse of knowledge and experience, he was capable of providing a few real surprises.

So Chung Ling Soo accepted the challenge of Ching Ling Foo. At the appointed time, eleven o'clock on the morning of

January 7, 1905, he arrived at the newspaper office in a big red automobile—a novelty itself in those days—wearing his Chinese make-up and mandarin regalia.

As a warmup, Chung worked a few close-up effects. He vanished a large Chinese coin with a hole in the center and caused it to reappear on a string, the ends of which were held by a newspaper reporter. He borrowed a cigar from an editor and pushed it down into a glass tube that he covered with a handkerchief. The cloth was instantly whisked away and the cigar was gone.

From Chung's inscrutable smile, the onlookers decided that Ching, when he arrived, might find it difficult to duplicate those tricks. But Ching Ling Foo did not come, and by noon it was plain that he had given up the challenge. Chung Ling Soo performed a few more tricks, finally somersaulting on the floor, and coming up with a glass bowl brimming with water and teeming with goldfish, a feat that Ching Ling Foo had never done. Then Soo departed, the winner by forfeit of five thousand dollars.

However, the money was never paid. The next day, Ching Ling Foo reissued his challenge, but with a new stipulation. Before he would deign to match magic with Chung Ling Soo, he insisted that his rival pay a visit to the Chinese legation and furnish proof that he was actually Chinese. Otherwise, the offer would be withdrawn.

In short, Ching Ling Foo was branding Chung Ling Soo an impostor, hoping, perhaps, to end his mandarin masquerade and put him out of business. Though the British public had been almost completely gulled by Chung's clever impersonation, various people in theatrical circles, particularly magicians, had long been aware that Chung Ling Soo was really Billy Robinson. Such rumors had unquestionably reached Ching Ling Foo, who had good reasons of his own to denounce Chung as a fraud.

But the exposure backfired. Chung Ling Soo was always

good copy for the British press, with his claims of mandarin ancestry and his defiance of the Boxers. They had admired his ability to turn reality into the fanciful. Now he came up with the most fantastic tale of all, the simple frank and unvarnished truth.

All his stories of China could be written off as publicity, because he had never been there. Actually, he wasn't even a Chinese, he was an American. Here was a case where fact was definitely stranger than fiction. The name Chung Ling Soo, translated freely, spelled William Ellsworth Robinson. In revealing his true identity, Robinson admitted that he had hoaxed the public, but in the same breath he defended his right to do so.

Millions of people had regarded his magic as the result of Chinese cunning; now, they realized that it was Yankee ingenuity. They had admired his apparatus as something that only Oriental craftsmen could have fashioned; instead, it was the product of British workshops. But above all, he maintained that it was a conjuror's business to deceive his audiences and they constituted his public.

Chung Ling Soo had done that in a way no one had ever attempted before. He had achieved an aim beyond all comparison. He could not have timed his triumph better if he had planned it. The name Chung Ling Soo was known throughout England. Vaudeville-goers in every city regarded him as the greatest magician of his day. Now he was also heralded as one of the most remarkable impersonators ever seen on any stage.

Chung Ling Soo played a solid three months at the Hippodrome and then toured England to bigger and better audiences than ever before. Ching Ling Foo and his troupe headed for America after closing at the Empire, and did big business throughout the United States, where his rival, Chung Ling Soo, had never appeared in the guise of a Chinese wizard.

British newspapers made many quips over the controversy,

carrying such headlines as: "Can Foo Fool Soo? Will Soo Sue Foo?" But the excitement was soon forgotten, and—oddly enough—the British public gradually forgot that Chung Ling Soo was really an American named Robinson. Never again did Ching and Chung cross paths.

In 1909, Chung Ling Soo made a world tour and on his return played his usual vaudeville circuits, season after season, on into the days of World War I, continually adding new illusions to his show, or reviving those that were popular favorites.

The "Bullet Catching Trick" always created a sensation when Chung presented it. Audiences found it particularly intriguing during World War I because soldiers invariably came up on the stage to examine the guns and load them, thus giving the act an added authenticity. Such was the case on the evening of March 23, 1918, when Chung Ling Soo appeared before a capacity Saturday night audience at the Wood Green Empire Theatre, in the northern section of London.

The act proceeded in its usual smooth fashion. Little Dot, appealing as ever in the make-up of Suee Seen, brought the marked bullets from the audience to the stage. There, two khaki-clad British soldiers, home on leave from France, loaded the antique rifles and turned them over to the Boxer firing squad. The theater grew tense as Billy Robinson, now a man in his late fifties, faced the guns in the impassive, impenetrable style characteristic of the Chinese wizard whose name he bore and whose regalia he wore.

It was a singular scene indeed. Across the English Channel, thousands of men were dying to the tattoo of machine guns in the barbed-wire no man's land between the Allied and German trenches, while miles of great cannons, placed wheel to wheel, stubbornly pounded the opposing lines, to the accompaniment of shrapnel bursts. Even here in London, any moment might bring the shrill of sirens and the muffled thun-

127

der of bombs, announcing a new air raid by the dreaded dirigibles, the German Zeppelins.

But, for the moment, the dozens of soldiers in the Wood Green Empire had forgotten the battlefields of France, while the rest of the audience were heedless that their own lives were in constant jeopardy. They were awed by the threat to Chung Ling Soo, accepting his artful pretense as stark reality, ignoring the fact that he had advertised and presented this same pantomime thousands of times during a span of eighteen years.

The rifles cracked; the audience gasped; and with that, the spell was broken. Tonight, Chung Ling Soo did not reel back; instead, his body jolted. His arm began its sweep, then dropped; the plate he held as target fell from his nerveless hand and shattered upon the stage. The magician slumped forward and sprawled across the fragments.

Quickly, the curtains closed, this time upon a tragedy. Something had gone wrong with the infallible bullet-catching act. The charge from one gun had struck the magician close to the heart, mortally wounding him. He was rushed to a hospital, but it was too late. By dawn, he was dead.

At the inquest, held a week later, the full secret of the "Bullet Catching Trick" was revealed. When Suee Seen received the marked bullets, they were placed in a special Chinese cup that had an inner wall, or lining. A space beneath the lining contained two duplicate bullets. On the way up to the stage, the diminutive assistant secretly removed the lining with the marked bullets and concealed it in the folds of her Chinese robe. Thus the bullets that the committee received from the cup were the duplicates, bearing marks that the committee supposed had been made by persons in the audience.

Suee Seen then went offstage, took the marked bullets from the lining, placed them beneath the plate and brought it on to Chung Ling Soo. Under cover of the plate, the bullets were slipped from her hand to his, so that he was all set to "catch" them later, simply dropping them on the plate when he gave his arms a sweep.

Many magicians used a similar type of "switch" and were therefore familiar with that part of the trick, but what baffled them was the loading of the guns. The duplicate bullets were *not* dummies, nor wax imitations. Magicians as well as soldiers had frequently gone up on the stage when the interpreter had called for a committee. They were sure that the loaded bullets were real.

In older versions of the trick, magicians had actually loaded guns, then secretly removed the bullets with the aid of a faked ramrod or some other mechanical device. But not so with Chung Ling Soo. The long ramrods were used by the committee and were examined before and after the loading operation, remaining in the committee's hands throughout, if so desired. As for the guns, the fact that they were really fired seemed to exclude any trickery there.

Yet the guns were tricked, and so ingeniously that the act seemed not only baffling, but safe. At the breech, or firing end of the gun, the barrel was blocked off with a solid plug of steel. When powder was poured in from the muzzle end, it was stopped by the plug. The bullet and wadding could be rammed home, because the charge was not fired; the firing pin could not explode it.

Beneath the barrel was a long tube containing the ramrod, a common feature of old rifles. Ingeniously, Chung Ling Soo had converted this into another gun barrel. A hole had been drilled down through the breech block to reach this secret barrel, which was loaded before the trick with a blank charge of powder and wadding only. This was jammed home with the wadding, which was left in place.

Each gun was examined in that condition. The ramrod was drawn out and used to load a real bullet into the actual barrel. The ramrod was then laid aside or left with the committee. When the trigger was pulled, the firing pin detonated the charge in the lower barrel only. The result was a burst of flame that appeared to come from the gun muzzle, but actually spurted from the open end of the long ramrod tube. The real load remained unfired and as each Chinese marksman went offstage with his gun, Chung Ling Soo had the marked bullets examined and returned to the audience. The duplicate bullets were removed from the gun barrels later, with the unfired charges. Before the next show, Chung Ling Soo inspected the rifles and prepared them personally. With such precautions, the trick apparently could never go wrong. But it did.

Over the years, a screw that held the steel plug in one gun had gradually corroded. Grains of powder had filtered down through the block from the rifle barrel, with its real load, to the disguised ramrod tube, with its blank charge. On the fatal night, the trickle was just sufficient for the lower charge to ignite the one above. Both fired simultaneously and the bullet found a human target.

Singularly, the career of Chung Ling Soo began as the result of a trick that went wrong, when the bowl of water spilled over the footlights and showered the orchestra at the Folies Bergère. It ended when another trick failed, on the stage of another theater, the Wood Green Empire, eighteen years later.

Chapter 6

THURSTON

(1869–1936)

All during the summer of 1876, people everywhere in the United States had been looking at big posters advertising the Centennial Exposition in Philadelphia. Now those were gone, at least in one city, Columbus, Ohio. There, a mysterious face peered from store windows, from building walls, even from the pages of the daily newspapers. The dark eyes beneath bushy brows were hypnotic in their gaze, and the mustache and goatee added a satanic look. Under the portrait was the announcement:

HERRMANN THE GREAT
CITY HALL THEATRE
THIS WEEK ONLY

Other lithographs depicted the master magician performing some of his marvels, which made people all the more eager to see the show. That applied particularly to a seven-year-old boy named Howard Thurston, who had saved up the pennies that he made from selling newspapers until he had enough to pay for the cheapest seat in the top gallery on the final night of Herrmann's engagement.

What a thrill that was for a boy who had never seen a show before, let alone a magic show! There was magic in the rising of the curtain, in the dancing of the gaslit footlights, in the dreamy music of the orchestra. Then the Great Herrmann strode onstage, removed his white gloves and rolled them into a bundle that he tossed above the heads of the audience. In mid-air, the gloves changed into a pair of white doves that soared back to the stage and alighted on the waiting hands of two assistants.

From then on, Herrmann performed one miracle after another. He produced fish bowls, brimming with water, from beneath a shawl. He poured dozens of different liquors from one bottle. He made chosen cards rise from a pack that he placed in a goblet. He scaled cards out over the audience, clear to the gallery, where Howard tried to catch one as it skimmed by. He transformed a jar of ink into water, with live goldfish swimming in it.

Those tricks impressed Howard as much as the larger illusions, such as the "Decapitation Mystery," in which Herrmann cut off a man's head and placed it on a table, where it came to life and jested with the audience. In all, it was an evening of enchantment, an evening, indeed, that young Howard Thurston was never to forget.

A few years later, Howard became a newsboy on fast trains running from Columbus to Akron and Pittsburgh. Always, he hoped to see Herrmann's show again, but the satanic sorcerer did not happen to play any of those cities. Howard's interest in magic gained new impetus, however, when he came upon Professor Hoffmann's highly informative book *Modern Magic*.

Among the mysteries the book revealed was the "Ink to Water" transformation. The transparent jar was really filled with water at the start, but it looked like ink because of a black silk lining that fitted neatly inside it. The magician simply covered the jar with a handkerchief and whisked away the black lining with it, revealing water instead of ink.

The goldfish, which had been in the jar from the beginning, were an excellent touch; their presence at the finish seemed to prove that the transformation was accomplished through magical rather than chemical means. But Herrmann had demonstrated that the liquid in the jar was really ink, before he had made the transformation.

As Howard recalled it, Herrmann had dipped a playing card—the Ace of Diamonds—into the jar and had brought it out with the lower half blackened and dripping with ink. Afterward, he had used an ordinary soup ladle to dip out some of the ink and pour it into a small glass saucer, which an assistant had carried into the audience for inspection.

Professor Hoffmann explained those details, too. The Ace of Diamonds was actually two duplicate cards, pasted back to back. The rear of that double-faced card was blackened half-way up. The magician showed what was apparently an ordinary Ace, but in dipping it into the bowl he gave it a deft half-flip and brought it out with the other side in view, so that seemingly its "face" was freshly inked.

The ladle was not as ordinary as it looked. It had a hollow handle filled with ink, with an opening at each end. The upper hole was plugged with wax, so the ink could not flow. In dipping the ladle into the jar, the magician stopped before he reached the water level. He thumbed the wax from the hole at the upper end of the handle and the ink flowed from the lower hole into the bowl of the ladle. It was the real ink that he poured out for inspection.

During his years as a traveling newsboy, Howard had stayed away from home for long periods. In the spring of 1886, despite his keen interest in magic, he set out again, this time selling programs with a racing circuit. His motive was not strictly selfish, for he intended to send money home, but his mother was unhappy at this parting. She was deeply religious and felt that no good could come from her son's association with the racing crowd of that era.

Howard was old enough to take much of that to heart. In New York, he became ill and was forced to stay there while the races went on their way. He was lonely, friendless, with little money and no job. One night, he attended a revival meeting conducted by Dwight Moody, the famous evangelist, and was gripped by some of the fervor that his mother had always hoped he would gain. He decided to become a medical missionary, and enrolled as a student at the Mount Hermon School in Massachusetts. This was welcome news to his mother, who died a short time later.

While at Mount Hermon, Howard Thurston gave his first real magical performance. It included the "Ink to Water" transformation, as well as a version of the "Rising Card" trick that he had also found in Hoffmann's *Modern Magic*. For a supergruesome finale, Howard improvised a decapitation trick, patterned after Herrmann's, with a fellow-student as the victim. What it lacked in artistry, it made up in realism, for Howard squirted a few sponge-loads of red ink over the victim's shirt and collar while pretending to cut off his head.

There were other magical programs after that, but the "decapitation" was omitted, by request of the school faculty, who were concerned about fainthearted visitors. After graduation, Howard Thurston set out for Philadelphia, early in 1892, intending to enroll as a medical student at the University of Pennsylvania.

The train ride to Albany was something of a flashback to the old newsboy days. Howard was thinking of that, when he reached the Albany station and found that he had a few hours to wait before taking a train to New York, where he would change again for Philadelphia. So he strolled about the city, and from force of old habit, he looked for a Herrmann poster. To his surprise, he found one, then more, as colorful and resplendent as the sheets that had papered his home town of Columbus fifteen years before.

Howard decided to stay in Albany overnight and see Herrmann's show again. By now, Howard was so versed in magic that he expected many of Herrmann's methods to appear quite obvious. Instead, Herrmann's artistry, his technique, were so superb that Howard was transplanted back to his earlier boyhood. All the amazement that had swept him then, gripped him anew and left him breathless. With Herrmann, there was no such thing as trickery. It was all sheer magic.

That was Herrmann's last night in Albany, but Howard saw the magic maestro again the next morning, at the Albany depot. Herrmann was wearing a soft hat that half obscured his hypnotic eyes, but his Mephistophelean features showed above the fur collar of his coat. He was accompanied by Madame Herrmann, and after he had bowed her to a seat, he turned imperiously to the ticket window, where he shifted his gold-headed cane beneath his arm as he asked the time of the next train to Syracuse.

Howard heard the ticket agent say, "Eight twenty," and as Herrmann turned away, Howard pushed a twenty-dollar bill through the window, saying he wanted a ticket to Philadelphia. Back it came, with the change, but as Howard glanced at the ticket, he saw that it read "Syracuse." It was already 8:15 and an announcer was calling, "All aboard for Syracuse!" Howard saw the Herrmanns going through the train gate; on impulse he followed them and boarded the same train.

That incident shaped the career of Howard Thurston. In Syracuse, he attended Herrmann's opening performance and was even more fascinated than in Albany the night before. His mind was made up: he would become a magician, not a missionary. The next morning, Howard left Syracuse on a train for Detroit, where his father had moved and had married again.

There, Howard spent a few months practicing his magic until both his father and his stepmother expressed disapproval of his new ambition and insisted that he either take a steady job or start out on his own. Howard chose the latter course and joined a circus side show that needed a magician so badly that the manager was willing to take on a mere beginner. Soon, Howard was performing card and coin tricks, producing articles from borrowed hats, and featuring the "Ink to Water" transformation.

Howard's beginning was small, and his progress was slow and difficult. By the time he had saved enough money to buy a full-dress suit like the magician pictured on the side-show banner—whom he was supposed to be—the show went broke and he barely managed to save his magical props from the sheriff.

Getting new jobs as a magician proved simple enough, for Howard's work had improved and he had expanded his program with new effects, but times were uncertain and the jobs failed to last. A new form of entertainment called vaudeville was coming into vogue, and Howard hoped to enter that field as Thurston the Magician. However, he was totally unknown, having only a few years of side-show and dime museum experience as a background.

The best he could do was join a variety troupe that traveled by wagon train and stagecoach through the mining districts of Montana and Wyoming, played saloons and dance halls with occasional performances in Indian villages along the irregular route. It was a healthy outdoor life, but extremely rugged, with little promise of profit and even less of fame.

Yet in the tiny town of Boulder, Montana, Howard Thurston was to make a magical "strike" that brought him a greater fortune than if he had stumbled over an unclaimed gold mine.

The most popular number on Howard's program was the "Rising Card Trick," which he presented much as he had seen Herrmann perform it, using a method described by Professor Hoffmann. Beforehand, Howard prepared a special packet of seven cards. He cut a short slit in the top edge of the front card and inserted the knotted end of a thread. Then he ran the thread down under the second card, up over the third, down under the fourth, up over the fifth, down under the sixth and up over the seventh. The packet was laid face up on the table and covered with a handkerchief. The thread continued off beneath the rear curtain of the stage.

The second, fourth and sixth cards were to be the risers, say the Ten of Diamonds, Five of Clubs and Queen of Hearts. To make sure the audience selected them, Howard used a "forcing pack" consisting of duplicate cards of those three values, arranged in groups of seventeen each. He spread the top third of the pack so one person could take a card; the middle third for the next person; and finally the bottom third.

The chosen cards were, of course, the Ten of Diamonds, Five of Clubs and Queen of Hearts, and when they were replaced in the pack, Howard shuffled it, taking care not to reveal any of the faces. On the way back to the stage, he dropped the forcing pack in his inside pocket and brought out an ordinary pack instead. When he reached the table, he picked up the handkerchief with one hand; with the other, he set the ordinary pack face up on the seven specially threaded cards.

Howard used the handkerchief to wipe a stemmed goblet; then he stood the glass on the table, picked up the pack, bringing the threaded cards with it, and placed it upright in the glass. At his command, a hidden assistant pulled the unseen thread, and one by one, the duplicates of the chosen cards rose slowly from the pack and toppled over the edge of the goblet onto the table.

Such was the "Rising Card Trick" as Thurston originally learned it, and the trick is just as workable today. It can be performed without an assistant by attaching the long end of the thread to a tack at the back of the table; in that case, the magician makes the cards rise by moving slowly forward with the glass, drawing the thread taut as he advances. He then takes the pack from the glass, disengaging the knot and letting the loose thread drop on the table.

Thurston's audiences in Montana included gamblers, card sharps and others who appreciated any fancy work with cards, so naturally they liked the "Rising Card Trick." Often, they kept shouting for the cards to rise clear out of the pack, but they never did, because they couldn't; at least, not until that night in Boulder.

The theater there was a billiard parlor and gambling hall by day, and when show time came, the pool tables, roulette wheels and faro layouts were simply pushed aside to accomodate the audience. While Thurston was arranging his tricks backstage, a fight broke out in the gambling hall. A shot pinged through the curtain and shattered the glass that he used in the "Rising Card Trick." Without it, Thurston's feature trick was gone, as he had no other goblet of the exact size for a pack of cards.

Quickly, Thurston improvised a new method which he had been thinking about but had never tried. He eliminated the threaded packet entirely. Instead, he tied one end of a thread to a nail at the side of the stage, and ran the thread straight across the stage above the level of his head. On the other side he inserted a screw with a small eyelet and ran the thread down through it. He attached a fish weight to the end of the thread and let it dangle, keeping the thread taut.

Next, Thurston took three cards from his forcing pack, one of each variety. To the back of each card, he glued a little cardboard tab near the top edge, leaving the bottom of each tab free so it could serve as a hook. Thurston put the three hooked cards on top of his regular pack, which he pocketed as usual. By then, it was curtain time, but fortunately the new trick was ready.

That night, Thurston descended into the audience and forced three cards, switching packs on the way back, as with his regular routine. But instead of picking up a glass, he faced the audience and held the pack in his left hand, pointing upward, about waist high. He raised his right hand above the pack, snapped his fingers and called for a chosen card to rise, but no card came. The audience snorted with laughter and Thurston lowered his hand, gave the pack an annoyed tap and raised his right hand high above his head.

Again, Thurston commanded a card to rise, with no response. The laughter grew louder and more raucous as he lowered his hand to give the pack a few more taps. This time, unknown to the audience, Thurston's hand engaged the thread that crossed the stage above his head, bringing its center down to the pack. That same action drew the end of the thread upward, hoisting the dangling fish weight almost to the eyelet.

While squaring the upright pack with his right hand, Thurston hooked the thread beneath the loose end of the tab on the card at the back of the pack. He pressed his left thumb firmly against the back of the card, while his left fingers girdled the lower portion of the pack. He raised his right hand shoulder high, snapped his right fingers and released the threaded card with his left thumb.

Laughter changed to applause as a chosen card rose gracefully from the pack straight up to the magician's waiting hand. Casually, Thurston showed the card with his right hand and placed it on the front of the pack, facing the audience. In so doing, he brought the unseen thread down again, detached it from the hidden tab, and brought the thread in back of the pack, where he hooked it under the tab of the second card.

Again, Thurston raised his right hand, snapped his fingers, and released pressure with his left. Again, the fish weight dropped offstage, bringing up the thread with another card. The audience was applauding furiously by the time a third card made its mysterious flight. In replacing that card on the pack, Thurston simply released the thread entirely, so he could walk beneath it as he bowed his way from the stage.

From then on, Thurston's "Rising Card Trick" created a sensation wherever he presented it. After six years as a small-time magician, he began to attract the attention of Western vaudeville circuits. In October, 1898, Thurston arrived in Denver, Colorado, to present his act at the Alcazar Theatre, and he was intrigued to find the city billed with posters advertising the Herrmann show. The star was no longer Alexander Herrmann, but his nephew, Leon.

Between his own shows, Thurston went over to the Tabor Grand, where Leon Herrmann was appearing. There, he was studying the elaborate lobby displays when a tall, keen-eyed man recognized him as the young magician who was doing the card act at the Alcazar. The tall man turned out to be Billy Robinson, who was still stage manager with the Herrmann show. Thurston learned that Robinson had seen his act at the Alcazar and had told Herrmann about it. Leon was anxious to see the act himself, but was too pressed for time. The upshot was that Thurston agreed to present his sensational new "Rising Card Trick" for Herrmann and his company on their own stage before the evening show.

That was indeed a news story: a newcomer among magicians about to give a command performance for the successor to the greatest master of the craft. Thurston notified the city editor of the Denver *Post*, and he assigned a reporter to cover it. After finishing an act at the Alcazar, Thurston arrived at the Tabor Grand early enough to make his preparations in a rear corner of Herrmann's stage, with the thread running from the backdrop to a wing. All was ready when Leon emerged from his dressing room, but unfortunately, it was almost time for his own show to start.

As the orchestra began its overture beyond the curtain, Leon raised his hand as though to dismiss Thurston and his act. Then, with a shrug, he remarked that his own audience could wait and he told Thurston to go on.

Promptly, cards were chosen by members of the company, and the first card rose, while Leon watched with the air of a detective ferreting out a clue. The overture ended abruptly, and in the uneasy hush that followed, Leon's assistants began to move to their positions for the opening curtain. Leon beckoned them back as he gave the order to have the orchestra play the overture again. Evidently he was finding the card act very interesting, for he nodded for Thurston to proceed.

Thurston timed the next rise to a new burst from the orchestra, hoping that a sudden glare from the electric border lights would not reveal the cross thread. But there was enough distance to lend the necessary enchantment, for Herrmann's stage was as big as some of the pool halls that Thurston had played in Montana and the Herrmann troupe was larger than some of the audiences he had entertained.

When the final card rose to the strains of Herrmann's own "Magician's March," the troupe broke into applause that was interrupted by the excited company manager, who arrived backstage wanting to know what was holding up the show. Nonchalantly, Leon waved his assistants to their places and strolled to the wing, to be ready for his entrance. There, he complimented Thurston, saying that his rising cards were excellent and adding that he had never seen a trick quite like it.

Thurston was quick to ask Leon if the trick had mystified him. Leon hesitated momentarily, as though unwilling to admit it; then he gave a nod. The *Post* reporter was standing by. He had seen and heard all. The theater curtain was rising now, and Leon Herrmann was striding onstage to take his opening bow, while Thurston hurried from the stage door to overtake the reporter and make sure he had the details right.

Next day, the story of Thurston's triumph was headlined with his picture and the caption, "The Man Who Mystified Herrmann." Thurston bought dozens of copies and mailed them to theatrical agents, hoping for immediate bookings on the strength of his new fame, but none came. He worked his way East, alternating side shows with vaudeville, until he reached New York City. There, his talents still went begging, but he learned the reason why.

Sensational though Thurston's rising cards might be, it took more than one trick to make an act. Unfortunately, Thurston's other tricks could not approach the big feature. He needed something else, and it had to be with cards, to lead up to the climax. That was a problem indeed, and to solve it, Thurston visited all the magic shops in New York, including one run by a man named Otto Maurer in a basement store on the Bowery.

In Maurer's shop the customers were discussing a Mexican sleight-of-hand artist who made a card disappear by flipping it out of sight behind his hand and retaining it there by what they called "the backhand palm," a self-contradictory term, though it expressed the general idea. As a follow-up, the card was brought inside the hand, so the back could be shown, making the vanish complete.

In a cheap room that he had rented on Lexington Avenue, Thurston dabbled with the new sleight. He held a card upright between his right thumb and forefinger. With his little finger, he pressed the far corner against the tip of his third finger. Similarly, he pressed the near corner between his first two fingers. He stretched his fingers straight out, showing the inside of his hand, and the card was gone!

Bringing the card inside the hand required a reversal of the move, with the thumb holding the card in place while the fingers were doubled and then extended, sliding along the card to press the corners at the other end. The hand could then be turned to show the back; another reversal and the palm was again empty. This was more than just a backhand palm, it was a back and front palm that terminated with the card reappearing at the finger tips, springing there as though plucked from mid-air.

Both the vanish and the reappearance of the card were "covered" by an up-and-down motion of the hand, so that the "flip" escaped notice. Thurston soon found that he could vanish and reproduce several cards one at a time, and the effect was excellent. But in turning the hand to bring the cards from back to front and vice versa, they were apt to be seen, particularly from the side angles.

While practicing before a mirror, Thurston noted that when he swung his hand completely outside the mirror frame, the transfer could be made unnoticed. So he turned his left side toward the mirror and made the same sweeping motion, bringing his right hand behind his body. That covered the turnover from every angle, yet the hand was gone from sight so briefly that the move roused no suspicion whatever.

Soon, Thurston was showing his manipulations to theatrical agents, who agreed that his vanish and reproduction of a dozen cards was the novel type of opening that his act needed. He was booked at Tony Pastor's famous vaudeville house on Fourteenth Street with one assistant, a young Negro boy named George White, who brought on items needed in the act and handled details backstage.

The card manipulations won the audience at the start, for along with the amazing vanish and reproduction, Thurston included other surprises, such as pushing a card into his right elbow and having it appear in his right hand; and later causing a card to pass invisibly through his knees.

This was done with a duplicate card. He had an Ace of Spades in each hand; one in sight, the other back-palmed. Vanishing one card and producing the other simultaneously, Thurston apparently made a single card go through magical gyrations. At the finish, he back-palmed them both together, reproduced what looked like a lone Ace and dropped it on a tray that George held handy, leaving the audience utterly baffled.

With the "Rising Card Trick," Thurston provided another innovation. He let people call for any cards they wanted, while he ran through an ordinary pack, checking to see if the cards were there. In so doing, he brought the cards to the top of the pack; meanwhile, offstage, George was picking out the same cards from a special pack, all with tabs on their backs.

George brought the tabbed duplicates on a tray with a goblet and a handkerchief. Thurston secretly picked them up, added them to the regular pack and worked the usual rise. That, too, was improved, for George and another assistant handled both ends of the thread from offstage, letting the thread dip down when needed. At the finish, Thurston tossed the three ordinary cards into the audience, then scaled souvenir cards to all parts of the theater, the way he had seen the Great Herrmann do.

Thurston concluded the act with a comedy finish, inviting a spectator up from the audience to help. From the man's pockets, vest and coat collar, Thurston brought batches of playing cards, strings of silk handkerchiefs and a wash line of baby clothes. Finally, he reached down behind the man's coat and brought out a live duck which quacked and pecked at the victim's head as he dashed down into the audience with the duck snarled in his coat collar.

The packs of cards were in Thurston's own pockets at the start. He bowed offstage after the "Rising Card Trick" long enough to pick up the bundles of silks and baby clothes, which he placed beneath his coat. It was easy for him to palm cards and bring them from the man's pockets, leaving batches that he shook out later. During that process, Thurston "loaded" the handkerchiefs and the clothesline from his own coat into the spectator's.

By then, George again came onstage with the tray to receive the articles that Thurston produced from the man's coat. Toward the finish, Thurston turned the volunteer fully around, so that his back was toward the audience, and at the same time, he drew the man's coat wide, dragging him in George's direction. On George's back was a knapsack, unseen by the audience, and it contained the duck. With his free hand, Thurston transferred the duck bag from George's back to the victim's coat. Once the bag was safely there, Thurston swung the man around again, working the bag beneath the back of his coat. Thurston then pulled a zipper device and the duck came up from behind the volunteer's coat collar.

The act ended with a riot of laughter and proved a great success on Thurston's first big-time vaudeville tour. Soon he was booked to appear in England, where novelty acts were in great demand. He opened a four weeks' engagement at the Palace Theatre in London on November 12, 1900, which proved to be one of the greatest nights in his career.

Thurston was nervous when he walked onstage, though his assistant, George White, was as cool as ever; but the applause that followed his card manipulations promptly restored Thurston's confidence. The "Rising Cards" won more enthusiasm, and when Thurston began throwing out souvenir cards, a remarkable thing happened. The applause became louder as the audience shouted, "More! More! Higher! Higher!" accepting the card-throwing as the feature of the act.

Thurston gave George a quick nod and the alert assistant brought on a trayload of throwout cards. Over the years, Thurston had acquired the knack of throwing cards, and now he put it to good use, scaling his souvenir cards to the deepest reaches of the uppermost gallery. Nothing like it had ever been seen before at the Palace, and when Thurston bowed off, exhausted, he smilingly told George:

"We won't need the duck trick tonight."

They didn't need it that night, nor any night during the engagement at the Palace, which was extended from four weeks to twenty-six. Following that, Thurston played vaudeville houses throughout England and then toured Europe. Language was no barrier in his case, as he only talked during the "Rising Card Trick," when he called for names of cards; by learning their foreign equivalents, he had all he needed.

Upon his return to America, in May, 1902, Thurston invested all his profits in an elaborate vaudeville act that required nearly a dozen assistants including George White. He appeared in a Persian military costume before an Oriental setting, and followed his card manipulations with a series of highly surprising effects.

One was the production of fire bowls instead of the usual

fish bowls. These were skillfully brought from beneath the magician's costume and ignited automatically when raised to a horizontal position. Thurston also produced live pigeons from a hat, instead of the customary rabbits, and then toy balloons that appeared fully inflated. This neat trick was accomplished by means of two chemical compounds inside the balloons.

Thurston's "Flowing Coconut" was also a surprising illusion. On the stage was a huge bowl, the size of a large tub. Into it, Thurston dipped a coconut shell from which he poured water back into the bowl. He repeated this more rapidly and finally inverted the coconut completely, holding it steadily above the bowl. By then, an inexhaustible stream was gushing from the coconut, filling the bowl and cascading over its rim into a series of basins.

The secret was indeed ingenious. A hidden pipe came up through the stage and into the bowl. As Thurston sped the pouring, he lowered the coconut toward the bowl; and when he inverted the shell, he gave the cue to turn on pressure from below. A jet of water shot up through the pipe to the shell, spread around the sides and showered downward. The descending water hid the upward stream, so the deluge seemed to come from the coconut itself, and varicolored lights added a resplendent effect. After the water was cut off, Thurston showed the coconut shell to be quite ordinary.

By 1905, Howard Thurston was in his mid-thirties, and his ambition, more than ever, was to have a show as great as Herrmann's. There no longer was a Herrmann show, for Madame Herrmann and Leon had gone their separate ways, though each was appearing in vaudeville. But Kellar had taken over in Herrmann's stead and Thurston knew it would be difficult to compete with him. Instead, he decided to embark upon a world tour, hoping to come back famous in his own right. Magic was popular in Australia and he figured that a big show might do well there. Once again, Thurston staked his profits on a new venture. He set out by steamship from San

Francisco with George White and a few other key assistants, along with all his props and baggage. His show proved a success in Australia and he continued on through the Orient.

But in India, luck turned against him. Business fell off because of a plague and Thurston was wondering where to go next when he received a cable from Kellar, offering him a part interest in the show. Kellar, it seemed, was looking for a successor and had heard of Thurston's earlier triumphs in the Far East. So Thurston headed home to America by way of England. In 1907, he combined his show with Kellar's and they worked together during one full season, after which Thurston took over the entire show.

For Thurston, that was a new beginning. Season after season, he increased the size of his show until it became the biggest magic show ever. He gradually eliminated all of the smaller or cheaper theaters that Kellar had played, until his itinerary matched those of the road companies of Broadway shows and musicals. That proved to be good judgment indeed. Vaudeville was still expanding and taking over the older legitimate theaters in many cities. Soon, huge movie palaces were to be built to supplant vaudeville, but by then, the Thurston show had become as much an American institution as the Ringling Brothers Circus or the Ziegfeld Follies, the great amusement enterprises of their era.

For more than twenty years Thurston toured the country with his show. Parents who remembered the Thurston show from childhood brought their own boys and girls to witness that same magic. Actually, though, it was never quite the same, because Thurston cannily added new tricks and bigger illusions to bring back his regular audiences year after year.

In his opening, Thurston always introduced rapid-fire surprises. His best was the production of a huge fish bowl which he caught beneath a large cloth and carried to a draped table at one side of the stage. The bowl was so heavy that he had to set it on the table before whipping away the cloth. It measured eighteen inches across and was six inches high, while the table was only fifteen inches square with a four-inch drape.

That apparently proved the bowl could only have come from the cloth, though actually it was in the table at the start. In arranging the table beforehand, the drape was folded up beneath it and fastened there by a special catch. The bowl was then placed on the table and covered with a dummy top, which was simply a thin square of hinged plywood that could be folded in half. The dummy top was larger than the bowl and it had a deeper drape, so the table looked quite normal.

Thurston pretended to catch a bowl under the cloth by forming a circle with his arms. When he reached the table to set the imaginary bowl there, he drew away the folding top beneath the cloth and released the real drape. He then stepped aside to reveal the bowl. While the audience stared in amazement, Thurston handed the cloth to an assistant who carried it offstage, the dummy top with it.

To top that mystery, Thurston produced a second bowl in the same fashion, setting it on a table at the other side of the stage. In his hurry, he spilled water on the way, and the audience assumed that he had tipped the bowl when catching it beneath the cloth. But the water didn't come from the bowl; it came from a fully saturated sponge stowed in the ornamental border of the heavy cloth. When pretending to catch the second bowl, Thurston squeezed the sponge. What appeared to be a near-accident was an added touch of deception.

The bowl production was not exclusively Thurston's. Other magicians performed it, usually with a single bowl, and they often criticized Thurston for producing two. Their argument was that after the first bowl had been produced, the audience could compare the tables—one with a bowl, the other without —and observe the difference in their sizes. To a shrewd observer, that would give the trick away before the second bowl was produced.

That was quite true, when performing on a small stage with the tables set well back and fairly close together. But Thurston worked on a large stage close to the footlights, where the tables were so far apart that comparison was all but impossible. Nor did Thurston give people time to think about such things during his fast-paced opening, in which one quick trick followed another in a way that left onlookers breathless. Usually, he had produced both bowls before anyone really began to study the tables.

Thurston slowed his pace in the next scene. To the strains of the "Zenda Waltz," the music he had first used at Tony Pastor's, he presented his famous card act, beginning with manipulations and following those with the "Rising Cards." At the finish, he scaled cards higher and higher as the orchestra played increasingly louder, drowning the shouts of the gallery patrons, who were waving for Thurston to skim cards their way. During his long career, Thurston probably threw out more than a million of his "good luck" cards bearing his picture; yet today, so few of them can be found that they have become highly prized collectors' items.

Another great feature of Thurston's first act was the "Levitation of Princess Karnac," the floating-lady illusion that he obtained from Kellar. After several seasons on his own, Thurston introduced a sequel to the levitation. Still hypnotized, the girl was brought from her couch by two assistants, and Thurston supported her with his outstretched arms while a large cloth was spread over her. Wrapped like a living mummy and surrounded by a committee from the audience, the princess was carried to the footlights, where Thurston suddenly crushed the cloth and flung it aside. In the matter of a mere instant, Princess Karnac had disappeared, seemingly transported back to her home in India.

This trick was accomplished by means of a hidden trap door. At the very moment when two assistants were stretching the large cloth, Thurston, half-kneeling on the stage, gave a quick cue and a trap door opened downward, letting him slide the girl through to the waiting arms of men beneath. The draped cloth hid the action, and all the while Thurston's head and shoulders could be seen above the upper edge. Moments later, he arose, apparently wrapping the sleeping girl inside the cloth, which really contained a flimsy wire form instead. By then, the trap door had closed and the illusion was as good as done.

Members of the committee did not surround the girl until she had been wrapped in the cloth, though if any of Thurston's friends happened to come up on the stage, they were allowed to stand behind him during the wrapping process. They saw the actual working of the illusion and at the same time could watch the intent faces of the audience beyond the footlights.

In later years, Thurston caused the draped form to rise in mid-air near the footlights and float above the steps leading down into the audience, at his hypnotic guidance. After that, he crushed the cloth, sending the girl on her invisible way. However, some critics felt that this detracted from the more convincing levitation illusion, where the audience saw the girl's visible form suspended in mid-air.

Novelty was the keynote of Thurston's second act. At one time, he engaged Theo Bamberg, an expert in hand shadows, to present that specialty. Other seasons, he introduced Hindu magicians who performed some of their celebrated tricks. When an Egyptian fakir called Rahman Bey arrived in America and demonstrated his power of suspended animation by allowing himself to be buried in a sealed coffin for a full hour, Thurston used one of his Hindu assistants to duplicate the feat.

Thurston hypnotized the Hindu and placed him in a glass casket which was submerged in a large tank of water with glass sides, enabling the audience to view the entranced victim in his airtight tomb. The tank was mounted on rollers and was moved to one side of the stage while Thurston continued with the second act. When the curtain fell, the tank remained in front with the submerged Hindu on display during the intermission. In the third act, the show was halted an hour after the burial had begun, and the sealed casket was hoisted from the water tank and opened.

The Hindu was brought from his trance by Thurston, and proved quite unharmed by his strange ordeal. The audience was bewildered, ready to accept suspended animation or hypnotism as the only possible explanation of the riddle. Yet actually neither factor was responsible. It was simply good showmanship on Thurston's part, plus the calm cooperation of the Hindu assistant.

The cubic capacity of the casket was larger than the audience supposed, allowing ample air to sustain the occupant for more than an hour, provided he breathed in slow, measured fashion, consuming a minimum of oxygen. This was tested beforehand, with the Hindu staying in the casket for short periods which were gradually increased, until an hour's stay became a mere routine.

When Thurston first presented the living burial, the casket was immersed in a swimming pool which was surrounded by a group of onlookers. Later, Thurston turned it into a vast outdoor spectacle, burying the Hindu alive in a solid coffin in the middle of a baseball park before thousands of spectators. The coffin was larger than the glass casket, providing enough extra air so that it could be lowered in a deep hole, covered with earth, and then dug up after the full hour had elapsed.

In the third and final act, Thurston presented many of the larger and more spectacular illusions that brought the public back to see his show, year after year. Frequently, he opened the act with "The Moth and the Flame," in which a huge, lighted candlestick was shown upon a platform supported by glittering metal rods, with an open space between it and the stage.

Half a dozen girls attired in winged costumes flitted about the platform like human moths. As each approached the candle flame, a circular canopy was lowered over her; when it was raised, the girl was gone. After the sixth girl had vanished, the audience was suddenly snapped from bewilderment by the sound of pistol shots behind them. As people turned, they saw the vanished moth-girls come dashing down the aisles with smoking guns, finally racing up onto the stage to take their bows.

The platform had five upright rods or legs, four at the corners, one at the center. It was set in a three-sided alcove with curtains at the sides and back. Two vertical mirrors ran from the center post of the platform to those at the rear corners. The mirrors reflected the side curtains, which were identical with the backdrop, so the audience supposed that when looking beneath the platform they could see the backdrop itself.

The huge candle was simply a half-shell fixed on the center of the platform. It hid an open trap forming a chute that went down behind the center leg and the V-shaped mirrors through another trap in the stage. As each girl was covered by the canopy, she stepped behind the candle and dropped through. With the last girl, Thurston always paused to address the audience before raising the canopy to show that she had vanished. That gave the group time to hurry out of the stage door and rush around to the front of the theater, to make their reappearance.

At one theater, the girls found a short cut through the basement to a downstairs smoking lounge, where a stairway led up to the auditorium. Before the curtain rose on an act, it was customary to sound a buzzer, or "call bell," in the lounge, giving people there sufficient time to get back to their seats, but one night, somebody forgot to ring the call bell. Twenty to thirty people were still in the smoke-filled lounge, when suddenly a door burst open and six girls in diaphanous costumes came dashing through the startled throng, brandishing revolvers. They raced on upstairs, and the crowd from the smoking room followed in time to see the mystery girls arriving on the stage to take a bow with Thurston in front of a huge candle.

That left the people from below more bewildered than ever, because they had no idea what had happened in the first place!

During other seasons, Thurston presented an illusion called "The Boy, the Girl and the Donkey." He brought all three onstage: a boy with a broad smile, a shy, demure girl, and a very balky donkey. They entered a curtained cabinet of large proportions and Thurston fired a pistol shot. When the curtain was whisked aside, the boy, the girl and the donkey had vanished.

The cabinet was deep, and just as the audience began to wonder whether or not they were still in it, the boy and the girl shouted, "Here we are!" from the back of the theater. They then dragged and shoved the donkey all the way to the stage, where they took their bows, while the donkey kicked its heels.

That really baffled audiences. People used to argue about it afterward. Maybe the cabinet did look big and tricky, but still the trio must have vanished from it. Otherwise, how could they have reappeared out in the theater? Of course, Thurston might have had a pair of twin boys, a pair of twin girls and a pair of twin donkeys, but that seemed wildly improbable.

And yet it was true. This was the actual answer to the mystery. While the original boy, girl and donkey were entering the double-backed cabinet on the stage, their identical twins were watching from the back of the theater, waiting for their cue to reappear, even though they had never vanished.

If the audience had looked around, they would have seen the twins too soon. Instead, they kept their eyes glued to the stage. That is the way with audiences; it is also why magic works. Studying such reactions was one of Thurston's fortes and he planned his show accordingly. Always, he varied his program so that each illusion provided a new surprise, and often he rearranged an old routine to make it appear new, or added an up-to-date twist.

An adapter rather than an inventor, Thurston frequently bought devices from other magicians, changing them to suit his needs. He was always willing to consider suggestions and advice, for he regarded magic as big business like any other theatrical enterprise. His skill was displayed chiefly in his card manipulations, but only because the trend was toward large, spectacular illusions, and it was his policy to set the pace.

Where other magicians injected dash and vigor into their presentations, Thurston depended on poise and deliberation. He seldom quipped with members of the audience, but he was masterful when it came to inviting committees up on the stage. Though his manner was restrained, he projected a sincere warmth and impressed onlookers with his somewhat ministerial air.

Thurston relied strongly on audience-tested features like his card act, the levitation, and the spirit cabinet, which formed high spots in his show. Each year he advertised new wonders, billing them as extravagantly as a circus, but the old reliables still swayed his audiences and brought back many of the same people each season.

Year after year, Thurston performed one great trick that began when the first spectators entered the theater and reached its climax at the very finish of the show. The arriving audience saw a large, squarish box hanging from the dome of the theater, attached to one strand of a double rope that ran over a pulley. The ropes came down to another pulley at the side of the stage, forming a continuous belt. People wondered why the box was up there, but they did not find out until the finale.

Then, assistants wheeled a big cannon on stage. A girl climbed a short ladder and slid down into the mouth of the cannon. Thurston aimed the cannon toward the dome of the theater and gave the order, "Fire!" There was a great blast and the mouth of the cannon was tilted toward the audience and shown empty as soon as the smoke had cleared.

The double rope was released and the box came sliding down the dome. The moment it reached the stage, it was opened and a smaller box was taken from within it. The second box was opened and a third box was lifted out and placed upon a pedestal. When this box was opened, out climbed the very girl who had been fired from the cannon.

Twins were no answer, as a girl could not remain cooped in the nested boxes all during the show. Moreover, Thurston quashed that theory by tying a borrowed handkerchief around the girl's arm before she was fired from the cannon. She was still wearing it when she emerged from within the triple boxes.

The girl's "invisible flight" was ingeniously accomplished. She slid out through an opening in the far side of the cannon and down through a stage trap before the cannon was pointed at the hanging boxes and fired. There were only two boxes in the hanging nest; the third—and innermost—was below stage. The girl was packed in it while the hanging pair was being brought down from the theater dome and set directly over the stage trap.

While the ropes were being detached, the box containing the girl was pushed up through the trap inside the other two. These had hinged bottoms that swung upward to receive the box with the girl. It was then simply a case of opening each box in turn so the girl could make her startling appearance.

In the early 1930s, Thurston introduced an illusion called "Iasia" in which a girl vanished from the dome of the theater. A girl garbed in a long Hindu robe stepped into a tall cabinet which was simply an open framework with a thin top and bottom. Four side curtains were pulled down and the cabinet was hauled up above the audience while the girl pushed lucky cards out through slits in the curtains, so they showered on the people below.

155

Weird, Oriental music increased the suspense until Thurston, standing on the runway, fired a pistol shot. Instantly, the curtains fell away, leaving only the empty framework. While the audience gaped in disbelief, Thurston spoke in a profound, dramatic tone:

"She is gone! Those from above can see that she is not in the top. Those from below can see that she is not in the bottom. She is gone, but there is no explanation. She is gone—just gone!"

That should have brought applause, but it failed to do so. The audience sat spellbound, unable to react. The illusion was so good, it defeated itself, and Thurston was forced to bow off amid unresponsive silence, until one night, a happy inspiration struck him. After a well-timed pause, he repeated:

"Yes, she is gone—just gone." Then he added: "And night after night, I stand here gazing up at that empty cabinet, wondering myself where she could possibly be."

That broke the ice. A ripple of laughter swelled into a peal of mirth which was followed by a spontaneous burst of applause. The idea of Thurston, of all people, being mystified by one of his own illusions, transported the audience from the miraculous to the ridiculous. That brought them to the balance point of true appreciation for the magician's art.

Actually, the girl went into the top of the cabinet. The "Iasia" illusion was a development of an older effect where a girl disappeared from a palanquin carried by two attendants. Weights, sliding down in the hollow posts of the frame, raised a double bottom nearly to the top, concealing the girl neatly and instantaneously.

In those days, you had to see it to disbelieve it. That empty, gleaming framework was proof in its own right. The distance and the angle left people doubting their own eyes. The result was, they agreed with Thurston. The girl was gone—just gone.

The "Vanishing Automobile" was another illusion that Thurston developed as a climax to his show. The curtain rose to reveal a triangular framework with upright slats or pickets. Above it was a sign that read: GARAGE. The back and sides of the stage had curtains with horizontal red and white stripes. The curtain on the right was lifted and a sports car rolled in view, carrying half a dozen passengers along with the driver. It stopped behind the slatted frame, with its occupants waving and shouting to the audience.

Then, Thurston took control. He fired a pistol, there was a great puff of light, and the sports car vanished. The audience could look right through the slats of the garage to view an absolute void!

This was another of the mirror illusions. With the puff of light, a whole series of hidden slats slid from behind the visible slats to fill the spaces between them. The hidden slats were composed of vertical mirrors that reflected the curtains at the sides of the stage. Since those curtains matched the backdrop, people still thought they saw straight through. As a result, the automobile apparently vanished.

Thurston spent small fortunes developing various new illusions; one of the most costly was his version of the "Indian Rope Trick." In this act, the curtain rose disclosing a large basket set in a tall, narrow archway at the back of the stage. At Thurston's command, a rope ascended slowly from the basket until its end reached the top of the arch, a dozen feet or more above the stage.

Next, a boy in Hindu costume climbed the robe and hung there, while powerful jets enveloped him with a blanket of steam, representing clouds of smoke from Oriental incense. As Thurston and a group of Hindu assistants gazed upward, the cloud cleared sufficiently for the audience to glimpse the boy, still clinging to the rope. A wave of Thurston's arms, and suddenly, the boy was gone, leaving only the suspended rope.

The secret was decidedly different from those of other stage illusions. The rope was drawn up by wires that were too thin to be seen against the darkened background, but were strong enough to take the boy's weight when he climbed to the top. As soon as the steam jets provided cover, the boy was hauled up into the flies, but meanwhile, a transparent movie screen rolled down to fill the curved portion of the archway.

From a rear angle, a hidden projector threw a lifesized color photo of the boy upon the screen. This was seen momentarily as the smoke cleared, giving a fleeting impression that the boy was still there. Then the projector blinked off, completing the vanish, and as the curtain fell, the spectators were staring at the bare end of the original rope through the transparent screen.

Clever though the "Rope Trick" was, it lacked the desired effect. If the projector clicked off too soon, the picture failed to register with the audience, and they assumed that the boy had scrambled away behind the smoke screen. If the picture stayed too long, it looked like what it was, a picture. So the success of the trick—when it did succeed—depended upon split-second timing.

Thurston featured the "Rope Trick" for a few seasons, getting the most out of the publicity that it brought, for feature writers and columnists were always ready to debate the "Rope Trick" pro or con, and it paid for itself on that score. But when the press notices lapsed, Thurston gladly dropped the "Rope Trick." It was one trick that proved just a bit too tricky.

Between seasons, Thurston developed and built new illusions in his extensive workshops at Whitestone, Long Island. The shops occupied the grounds of a small amusement park, which was surrounded by a high board fence, keeping it immune from the public eye. One of the buildings had a fully equipped stage on which new illusions could be tested and rehearsed after they were completed. The security measures around the workshop resembled those of a modern A-bomb project, as

Thurston did not want his next year's novelties to be copied before he could present them.

The old Herrmann mansion was a mile from the workshop, but Thurston was unable to buy it, since plans had already been made to demolish the building and erect an apartment house on the site. So Thurston bought a solidly-built stable that was on the Herrmann property and expanded it to an impressive home, with broad verandas opening onto shaded lawns and well-kept tennis courts. There he spent his summers and off-seasons for twenty years, from 1915 to 1935.

During most of those years, the Thurston show kept growing larger and larger, until it required a company of more than forty people and two baggage cars to carry the equipment. Storage houses in Whitestone were loaded with Thurston's older tricks, as many of them could be revived or redesigned after a few years.

Thurston's one great problem was theaters; with all his magic, he could not increase their size, and he often had to eliminate certain cities from his route because they had no theater big enough for his show. Either the stages were too small, or the auditoriums lacked the seating capacity necessary to make an engagement profitable. Still, these towns clamored for Thurston's magic, so he sent out a second company headed by a veteran magician named Jansen, who adopted the stage name of Dante. Most of Thurston's latest illusions were also featured in the Dante show, which in its turn grew so large that during the late 1920s, Thurston sent it on a tour of South America. From there Dante embarked for Europe on his own.

Meanwhile, Thurston had put together another company with a personable performer named Sugden starring under the billing of "Tampa, England's Court Magician." Later, Thurston's brother Harry formed a show quite similar to Howard's own, presenting it as Thurston's "Mysteries of India" and playing smaller cities.

The rise of the talking picture marked the decline of the legitimate theater, but the big movie houses were putting on elaborate stage shows in conjunction with their feature pictures. These presentations were about an hour long, so Thurston condensed his show to that length of time and continued to tour as a magician at the age of sixty-two.

The going proved more arduous than he anticipated. Already, he had lessened the strain of his full-evening show by introducing his daughter Jane to the stage as a *magicienne*, and the clever novelty acts that she presented gave Thurston longer rest periods during his regular performances. He thought that the one-hour presentations, in which Jane also appeared, would not be overtaxing. But he was wrong.

There were five such shows a day, and Thurston had scarcely recuperated from the strain of one, before another was due. After one season, he switched to radio for several months, presenting a dramatic show with magic as its theme. Soon, however, he was back at the five a day again, drawing a fabulous salary, but weakening more and more, though he masked that fact from his audiences, from his company, and even from himself.

In October, 1935, Thurston suffered a stroke shortly after completing the final show of the evening in Charleston, West Virginia. He recuperated gradually, and went to Miami, where, six months later, he had recovered so completely that he made a trip to Tampa to plan a new show with a mind reader named Rajah Raboid. By combining magic with mentalism, Thurston felt that they could draw big-enough crowds to warrant hiring their own auditoriums and going back to full evening shows.

Unfortunately, that hope came too late. On his return to Miami, Thurston suffered a second stroke and died on April 13, 1936, a few months before his sixty-seventh birthday. His funeral was held in Columbus, his home town, and it ended with a special ceremony in which a wand was broken above the magician's casket, to signify that his career was ended.

Nearly forty years before, Thurston had walked onstage at Tony Pastor's to give the performance that had started him on his road to fame. With him, he had just one assistant, a nine-year-old boy named George White. In all the years between, in every performance, great or small, that Thurston had ever given, George White had always been beside him. Often Thurston had said, "I've never given a show without George White, and I never will. Without George, my show just can't go on."

Fittingly, it was George White, now a man of nearly fifty, who stepped forward, this time alone, to perform the solemn rite of breaking the magician's wand.

One of Thurston's many "broadsides" issued during his years as America's best-known magician.

Chapter 7

HOUDINI AND HARDEEN

(1874–1926)   (1876–1945)

When Ehrich Weiss was nine years old, his father took him from Appleton, Wisconsin, to Milwaukee, where they attended the performance of a celebrated English magician who called himself Dr. Lynn. The big feature was an illusion entitled "Paligenisia," in which the crafty doctor strapped a man to a board and proceeded to dismember him, limb by limb, finally assembling the dismantled parts and restoring the victim to his original form.

This was one of the earliest of "torture illusions" in which later magicians were to specialize, and it had a profound effect upon Ehrich. He was impressed by the audience's reaction, too. He noticed how eagerly they watched, despite their horror. If something had gone wrong, they would have liked it. Then and there, Ehrich observed the effect of suspense upon the human mind, and he was never to forget its spell.

Back home, Ehrich learned a few small tricks from performers at circus side shows, and he hoped some day to acquire larger effects, like those presented by Dr. Lynn. He even traveled briefly with a circus as a boy acrobat and contortionist. He also worked as an apprentice for a locksmith and learned how to pick difficult locks and open handcuffs without keys.

In 1888, the Weiss family moved to New York City, and Ehrich, then fourteen years old, took a job as a necktie cutter in a factory at 502 Broadway, traveling between there and his home on East Sixty-ninth Street by the steam trains of the newly built elevated railway. Ehrich still wanted to become a magician, and very soon his ambition was furthered by two new friends.

At the next bench in the factory was a worker named Jack Hayman, who performed tricks like snapping coins up his sleeve, or finding cards that were chosen from a pack. Soon, Jack was teaching such hanky panky to Ehrich, and telling him about larger tricks that he had at home, and used when he put on occasional performances.

Ehrich didn't have much time to visit Jack right then. Summer was coming on, and Ehrich had been invited to join the Pastime Athletic Club, at Sixty-seventh Street and the East River, a few blocks from his home. The captain of the track team, Joe Rinn, was about four years older than Ehrich. One night, Joe surprised the new member by showing him some sleight-of-hand tricks that were as good as any performed by Jack Hayman.

From then on, Ehrich's progress in magic was rapid. What he learned from Jack Hayman, he used to baffle Joe Rinn, and vice versa. Finally, he let them both in on the secret and all three became good friends. But Ehrich profited most, for he gained the viewpoints of both.

To Jack Hayman, magic was a steppingstone to show business, where he felt he belonged. Joe Rinn, despite his youth, was already the owner of a fruit and produce market, and was studying magic to learn the methods of fake spirit mediums who were duping some of his wealthy customers. Listening to Hayman at work, and going around with Rinn during his spare time, left Ehrich with little to think about but magic.

Ehrich's big problem was buying tricks, for most of the money he made went to help support his family. He put on occasional shows with Jack Hayman, for which they collected fees that were invested in new apparatus; but mostly, Ehrich made up

163

tricks of his own, or practiced sleights that he learned from secondhand books. Anything connected with magic fascinated Ehrich, and that was how he happened to delve into an English translation of the *Recollections of Robert-Houdin.*

At first, Ehrich was disappointed, for he had hoped it would be a book of tricks. Then he became quite as enthralled as Houdin himself had been when he had picked up the wrong books at a bookseller's shop. At work, he kept telling Jack Hayman the things he had read, until, finally, his friend suggested that if he wanted to be like Houdin, he should take a suitable name. The best way would be to add an "i" to Houdin," forming "Houdini," which could be interpreted to mean "like Houdin."

The name appealed to Ehrich, as it gained a distinctive pronunciation. Where "Houdin" had the sound of "Hoo-dan," the name "Houdini," naturally became "Hoo-dee-nee." Ehrich thanked Jack for the suggestion and said that he would use it. When Ehrich next met Joe Rinn, he announced that he was going to quit his job and do a magic act under the name of Houdini.

Rinn advised against it, particularly when Ehrich added that he intended to follow the style of Robert-Houdin, as the name indicated. The name sounded good to Rinn, but that form of magic was outmoded. Rinn felt that Ehrich had been reading the wrong book. In place of the *Recollections of Robert-Houdin,* Rinn gave Ehrich a volume which had just been published and which represented the modern trend.

The book was entitled *Revelations of a Spirit Medium* and it proved to be exactly that. The author, who was careful not to divulge his name, had been fooled by fraudulent mediums and had tried to develop psychic powers of his own. When it dawned on him that the whole thing was a fake, he worked a few crude tricks on his fellow-believers to see if he could impress them.

They were so convinced he was real that he became a

professional medium and soon was exchanging ideas with others in the game, until he decided to give it up and expose the racket. This book was the result and it sounded very authentic to Ehrich, particularly when the author stated that anyone could spend a hundred dollars at a magical supply house like Martinka's in New York, without learning the secrets in his book. Joe Rinn had bought a thousand dollars worth of tricks from Martinka and Company. Ehrich knew how they all worked and both he and Rinn agreed that the tricks in the book were better.

The book described how mediums could slide in and out of knotted ropes without untying them. So Ehrich and Rinn began tying each other up to see if it worked. Both were athletes with big muscles and large chest expansion, which helped them to gain slack while being tied. They soon found that they could escape from any bonds, as the book said.

Sometimes ropes were tied to ringbolts set in the woodwork of the medium's cabinet. The book showed how such bolts could be secretly unscrewed, enabling the medium to produce his manifestations. There was also a special pillory that encased the medium's neck and wrists. It was secured by a formidable padlock, but that did not trouble the medium. The pillory had a trick hinge that opened at the other end.

In reading of such devices, Ehrich became more and more convinced that some unfathomable escape would be a sensation as the climax of his magic act. Through judicious inquiry at Martinka's, he learned of a man named Sylvestre in Chicago who furnished mediumistic appliances to confidential customers. One such item was a combination escape trick in which a person was tied inside a sack and locked in a trunk, only to change places almost instantly with another person on the outside.

The exchange took place under cover of a curtained cabinet. A trick sack and a trunk with a secret panel accounted for the mystery, but both could be thoroughly examined by a committee. The same applied to special handcuffs, also sold by Sylvestre, enabling the performers to switch those, too. The only problem was the price. Sylvestre wanted fifty dollars with the handcuffs extra. But once on the trail of the sack and trunk, Ehrich learned of a performer who had an old outfit for sale cheap, so he bought it.

There still was one difficulty. To work the sack and trunk substitution, Ehrich needed a partner. So he urged Jack Hayman to quit his job, too. As the Houdini Brothers, Harry and Jack, they could both work magic and finish with the trunk trick. Jack finally agreed, and on Friday, April 3, 1891, Ehrich Weiss left the factory and started out to book engagements for the Houdini Brothers.

Monday, April 6, was Ehrich's birthday. He was just seventeen years old, and on that day, he took the stage name Harry Houdini. He was never to change it, and eventually he had the name legalized as his own.

The partnership of the Houdini Brothers did well for a time, but did not last long. To make the act look right, one had to be the magician, the other the assistant. Harry was dynamic even at seventeen, and as he gradually took charge, Jack became dissatisfied and dropped out, turning the job over to his younger brother, Joe Hayman, who was willing to be a mere assistant.

So the Houdini brothers became Harry and Joe, until Joe Hayman turned comedian and branched out on his own. Harry then took his own younger brother Theo into the act and by the summer of 1893 they had saved enough money from their performances around New York to go west to Chicago and try their luck at the big Columbian Exposition.

That took daring, for their act was strictly small time. Harry, attired in a dress suit with black vest, bow tie and wing-tipped collar, looked quite confident as he strode on stage, and his black, bushy hair captured immediate attention. Theo, whose dashing manner had gained him the nickname

"Dash," had some difficulty keeping in the background, for he was taller than Harry and was assertive in his own right. But Dash was willing to follow Harry's lead and together they were a perfect team.

Most of Harry's tricks, however, were stock stuff. At one time, he opened the act by waving his hand over his buttonhole and causing a rose to appear there. The artificial flower was originally under his left arm and was whipped into place by a thin black elastic strip running through the buttonhole.

Another of Harry's favorite tricks was to show both hands unmistakably empty, then pick up a match box, light a candle, and immediately pluck a silk handkerchief from the flame. The tightly rolled silk was wadded in the back portion of the half-opened wooden match box. The natural act of closing the drawer before striking the match secretly ejected the handkerchief into Harry's palm, ready for the subsequent production.

Occasionally Harry worked a "Wine and Water" routine and even such stand-bys as the "Die through Hat," the "Bran Glass" and the "Watch Target," all items that were in every dealer's catalog and dated back a generation or more. But his "Dyeing Silks," which changed colors when he pushed them through a seemingly empty paper tube, were more up-to-date; and when he produced a large lamp on a table, it really surprised the audience.

The lamp trick was done with the aid of an unprepared cloth, so large that Harry and Dash had to spread it between them to show it empty. That left one of Harry's hands free just as the cloth was draped above the table and he neatly picked up the lamp, which was lying flat on a hidden shelf, and set it upright on the table before he whisked the cloth away.

Harry also did fancy knot work with silk handkerchiefs and performed some excellent card sleights, which he concluded by throwing the pack at a large, nickel-plated device called the "Card Star." There, chosen cards appeared mysteriously upon the points. They were duplicate cards that sprang up from behind the center of the star when Dash pulled the hidden release offstage. And like most of the act, it looked too mechanical.

That did not apply to the "Sack and Trunk," which had been given the name "Metamorphosis" and was sensational enough to be an act in itself. But there were too many acts along the Midway, as the entertainment section of the world's fair was termed. Harry wound up doing a small magic act in a Chicago dime museum, while Dash went back home to New York.

Without Dash, there was no trunk trick, so Harry used the curtained cabinet to escape from ropes in which he was tied by a committee and from standard types of handcuffs. That was the real beginning of the career of Houdini, the handcuff king and escape artist.

When Harry returned to New York, he and Dash resumed the Houdini Brothers act. The popularity of the Midway at the Chicago Fair promised good business at all amusement parks, so they booked their act well ahead at the Sea Beach Palace in Coney Island during the summer of 1894. It went over big and the Houdini Brothers were planning for something still bigger, when fate intervened.

Harry met a charming, diminutive girl named Beatrice Rahner. They fell in love, and after a brief courtship they were married. Soon afterward, they decided to present their own act as Harry and Bessie Houdini. The next summer, they joined the Welsh Brothers Circus and worked the "Metamorphosis," while Dash stayed in Coney Island and put on an escape act of his own, appearing as Theo Houdini. On the road, Harry did the same, escaping from handcuffs as well as rope ties.

Escape acts dated back a century and more, for the Chevalier Pinetti had freed himself from chains attached to posts and had performed a version of the "Thumb-Tie Trick," all explained in a book on *White Magic* written in 1789 by the

French author Decremps. During the 1860s, the Davenport Brothers had slipped ropes while confined in their "spirit cabinet." In 1883, Professor Taylor of Boston had performed a "Box and Sack" mystery which was a forerunner of the one presented by the Houdinis. In his box trick, Taylor allowed himself to be locked in antique shackles from the New Hampshire state prison.

After his escape, Taylor was given the shackles as a reward, and he used them from then on, letting committees inspect them and make sure that they were genuine. That was but a step to the "challenge handcuff act" where local police were invited to bring their handcuffs on the stage and lock up the performer. Later, such challenges were extended to all comers, provided that their handcuffs were of regulation types.

In the 1890s it was common practice for manufacturers of safes, locks and handcuffs to challenge persons to try to open them, with a cash reward for anyone who succeeded. Repeated failures were a good advertisement for the lock manufacturers; and if anyone did manage to crack their locks, they soon put out improved patterns that were guaranteed pick-proof—until some one did it again.

Thus, many "handcuff kings" of that era and later were simply skilled lock pickers who shrouded their performances with an atmosphere of mystery, usually by working within the confines of their cabinets. Being showmen, they resorted to trickery, and used fake cuffs whenever feasible, rejecting any that looked too formidable. Still, their ability was judged by their skill at picking locks and their knowledge of handcuffs generally.

Houdini started out along accepted lines, but during the six years from 1893 to 1899, he constantly expanded the scope of his act, accepting all patterns of standard cuffs, and even freak types, or antique irons. He offered rewards of gradually increasing amounts to any person who could handcuff him so he could not escape. He challenged police chiefs to lock him up in jail cells, and he broke out of those as easily as he shook off handcuffs.

That made it more difficult for rival handcuff kings, and many of them gave up the business. Some couldn't meet the more exacting challenges, while others felt it wasn't worth the effort for the money involved. The money bothered Houdini, too, for he was appearing chiefly in circus tents, dime museums and beer halls, where escape kings were classed with contortionists and acrobats. But he was gradually building his act into a real theatrical attraction.

During those years, Houdini also developed other types of escapes. He discovered that a standard packing case could be rendered vulnerable by removing a few long nails and substituting short ones. He let local concerns build such boxes according to his specifications, which included air holes so he could breathe while confined therein. When the box was delivered at the theater, Houdini or a helper always managed to arrange a brief opportunity to fix the needed nails.

Onstage, Houdini was roped or handcuffed and put in the box, after which the lid was tightly nailed in place. The curtained cabinet was lowered over the packing case; soon, Houdini emerged from the cabinet free. The cabinet was then raised and the packing case was found to be as tightly nailed as before.

The air holes actually helped in the escape, for by inserting his fingers in them, Houdini could swivel the loose boards inward. Before coming from the cabinet, he would put the long nails back in place, often driving them home with a hammer that was concealed in the cabinet. Any hammering sounds were drowned by the orchestra, which played loudly all during the act.

While Houdini was touring with a magician named Marco, the show went broke in Halifax, Nova Scotia. Houdini took over and tried all sorts of stunts to bring money into the box office. In St. John, New Brunswick, he accepted a challenge to escape from a type of strait jacket used to confine the criminally insane. Houdini's arms were encased in the jacket's long sleeves, which were stretched across his body and strapped behind him. Still, he managed to effect an escape.

Houdini's method was this: As with the rope ties, he stretched his muscular arms and swelled his chest, fighting for slack while being strapped. He gained enough to work one arm over his head; then the other. He then stepped through the dangling sleeves and brought the straps in front of him, where he worked them loose with his teeth.

When Houdini came from his cabinet carrying the jacket, gullible people believed he had accomplished the feat by spirit aid, whereas hardheaded skeptics insisted that the jacket was faked. To satisfy both classes of customers, Houdini worked that one escape in full view, letting the audiences witness his skill. He escaped from many strait jackets after that, some more formidable than the first, and the feat was so difficult that he had few imitators.

However, one escape that Houdini attempted while in Nova Scotia almost proved to be his last. Somebody brought up the story of Mazeppa, the Cossack leader who had been lashed to a horse which was driven out over the Russian steppes. Mazeppa, fortunately, had been rescued, but the question arose if Houdini—or anyone else—could free himself from such a plight.

Houdini was willing to try it, but specified that he must have a quiet, well-trained horse. Instead, he was given one that went wild and broke loose before he could begin to work free. There was Houdini, tied to a runaway horse, faced with the realization that if he partly released himself, he would be thrown to the ground and dragged to his death. Each time the horse slackened pace, Houdini's struggles urged it on again.

That gave Houdini one of the inspirations that seemed to come whenever he was in a tight spot. Carefully, he worked one hand free enough to find a rope end and used it to lash the horse into a still more rapid pace. The rest of the ropes held firm, and under Houdini's goading the unruly animal soon became so exhausted that it could run no farther. Then Houdini had his opportunity to extricate himself from the ropes without danger, for the horse was practically standing still.

Once, when business was bad, Houdini had just enough money to buy tickets for himself and Bessie to reach the next town with their baggage. The train was late and when they changed to another at a junction, they found it ready to pull out before their baggage was transferred. Houdini objected, but the conductor told them not to worry, adding that their baggage would come along on a train tomorrow.

Tomorrow, and their act was tonight! Harry told Bessie to get the baggage transferred while he pleaded with the engineer. But the conductor's word was law and the engineer would not listen. Houdini then raced up the track and laid himself across the rails, locking his arms to one and his legs to the other.

Naturally, the engineer couldn't start the locomotive, so the angry train crew tried to pry Houdini loose. He hung on grimly until Bessie arrived with word that the friendly station agent had put their baggage on the train. Houdini arose, grinned, and offered to shake hands with the train crew. He and Bessie boarded the train and worked their act that night.

Still, the act was getting nowhere. In the spring of 1899, they were working a dime museum in Minneapolis, wondering where they would go next, when Houdini's handcuff act caught the attention of Martin Beck, head of the Orpheum vaudeville circuit. He booked the Houdinis as a novelty act, to open in San Francisco in July. This gave Houdini a chance to arrange a big publicity stunt which really put the show across.

Occasionally, Houdini had augmented his handcuff act by visiting local jails and offering to escape from a locked cell. These escapes, too, depended upon his knowledge of locks and his ability to smuggle a pick or suitable key into the cell. Houdini was skilled at that and added to the mystery by allowing himself to be thoroughly searched before making the test. It proved a sensation in San Francisco, and when one newspaper tried to explain the jail escape, Houdini repeated it and completely baffled the reporters.

As champion jail breaker and handcuff king combined, Houdini headed east on the Orpheum circuit, scoring a success in every town he played. He and Bessie were still working the "Metamorphosis," but the rest of the act consisted of the handcuff challenge. Jail escapes brought big headlines and Houdini was confident that he would be booked immediately by big vaudeville houses in the East.

He was, but not for the long run that he hoped. The jail escapes didn't create the immediate stir that they had out West, where people still recalled the period of famous outlaws. Again, Harry and Bessie saw their savings dwindle, until Houdini resolved to gamble what was left and go to England, where novelty acts were in great demand. The Houdinis arrived in London in June, 1900, just one year after they had started out so hopefully in San Francisco. But there they had been booked; here, they were not.

Through an enterprising agent named Harry Day, Houdini was offered an engagement at the Alhambra Theatre, provided he could convince Scotland Yard of his ability as an escape king. Accompanied by Dundas Slater, manager of the Alhambra, Houdini called on Superintendent Melville at the Yard, and was promptly "fitted" with a pair of late-model English handcuffs.

Houdini was prepared for that. With a few deft moves, he shook off the handcuffs, leaving Melville amazed. That satisfied Slater, and Houdini opened at the Alhambra. Capacity audiences greeted every show. From England, Houdini went to Germany, creating an even greater sensation there. Both countries already had so-called "handcuff kings," but their knowledge was limited and they depended greatly on faked cuffs. Houdini met their challenges, but they refused to accept his, which added to his fame.

Soon, German theaters were invoking holdover clauses to prevent Houdini from playing other engagements that he had already booked. Houdini wanted to get back to England before new imitators could capitalize on his reputation; but he knew that the moment he left Germany, others would flood that country. Getting out of the dilemma was truly a job for an escape king. Houdini solved the problem by sending for the one man who could put on an act like his own, his brother Theo.

Dash had been out of show business for a few years, but when he received a cable from Harry saying "Come over, the apples are ripe," he took the next boat. A complete act was waiting when he reached Berlin. There were handcuffs, all the implements, stage sets, a replica of the substitution trunk, even bookings, some in opposition to Houdini's own. On that account, Houdini had given Dash a new name: Hardeen.

To cover the fact that they were brothers, Hardeen was billed as an English escape king, since Houdini was known to be an American. Thus they were able to pose as rivals when the occasion demanded, but meeting competition was their primary goal. After Houdini finished his return engagements in England, he resumed his intended tour of Europe. Hardeen promptly appeared in England and was so successful that he received seven years of solid vaudeville bookings. During five of those years, Houdini appeared chiefly in Europe, but played occasional engagements in England, where the field was big enough for both his own act and Hardeen's. In the fall of 1905 he returned to America, and presented his challenge handcuff act for several highly successful seasons.

The great secret of the "challenge" handcuff act was the proviso that "regulation" handcuffs be used and that they must be in proper working condition. Though there were dozens of regulation makes, such as Bean Giants, Plug Eights, Pinkertons, Towers and Scotland Yard Adjustables, both Houdini and Hardeen had familiarized themselves with all types.

They also traded on the fact that all handcuffs of a specified pattern are usually made to open with the same key, something that few people realize. This makes it easy to send prisoners from one place to another and unlock them at the other end. It also helped the handcuff kings, back in their palmy days, as all they needed was a complete set of regulation keys to be ready for the average challenger.

However, the fewer keys the better. Houdini devised some special keys that would unlock handcuffs of several different patterns. There was also the problem of getting the key to the keyhole while handcuffed. Often, Houdini held the key in his teeth and brought the handcuffs to it. He also invented curved rods, or "reachers," in which a key could be fixed in order to approach the keyhole.

When challengers came onstage, Houdini asked to examine the cuffs they brought. He tried these with their keys, to make sure that they worked. If he came across outmoded cuffs, he sometimes rejected them, but usually he had ways of handling those as well as regulation types. Knowing what keys were needed was the first step; getting them into the cabinet, the next.

Most escape kings concealed their keys somewhere on their person, a favorite device being a leg belt, like a garter, fitted with key pockets and worn just below the knee. Houdini recommended concealing keys in the cabinet itself, the best place being the hollow metal tubing of skeleton framework, which was cut away at the back curtain. One handcuff king even had his initials sewn in broad, gold braid on the inside of the rear curtain. Those ornamental letters were really pockets into which assistants slipped required keys.

In addition to master keys, Houdini and Hardeen used

special picks. One was a simple strip of steel, three and one-half inches long and only one-quarter inch wide, that could be pushed under the ratchets of a handcuff. This could spring all ratchet cuffs except types with double locks, which had to be opened with keys.

With freak handcuffs, Houdini, deft at sleight of hand, sometimes switched the real key for one that resembled it. Instead of giving the false key to the owner of the cuffs, Houdini would hand it to another member of the committee. He would take the real key into the cabinet with him, use it to open the cuffs, and switch it back later. In some cases, he slipped the real key to an assistant, who took it backstage and stamped out a duplicate on a special machine that Houdini carried with the act.

Houdini's surest way of dealing with formidable cuffs was to have his wrists locked with four or five pairs of handcuffs, one above the other. The difficult pair was always placed highest up, clamped to Houdini's forearms, which were so much thicker than his wrists that he could simply slide off the troublesome cuffs after unlocking those below.

On his return to America, Houdini encountered rival hand-cuff kings, some of whom—including such capable performers as Brindemour, Cunning and Raymond—had good claim to the title, having gained fame at home while Houdini was winning most of his abroad. The feuds that resulted would make a chapter in themselves, but they faded as the popularity of the handcuff act faded.

When this happened, about the year 1908, Houdini was forced to turn to other escapes. It was then that he devised his famous "Milk Can Escape," a really baffling mystery, yet one that was sure and certain, as Houdini insisted all good escapes should be.

This escape, as presented first by Houdini and later by Hardeen, required a huge, specially constructed milk can which was examined by members of the audience, then filled with water. Houdini, attired in a bathing suit, entered the milk can and its top was clamped down, locked with padlocks and covered by the cabinet. After a few suspenseful minutes, Houdini appeared from the cabinet, dripping with water. The milk can was still padlocked and could again be examined.

Houdini used several styles of milk cans: some broke open at the shoulder while others had an outer neck that slid up, carrying the padlocks with it. All would stand full examination, since the only way to work them was to get inside and ram the top portion upward. Even if a committeeman had tried that, he would have failed, because the milk can needed the added weight of the water to anchor it when its occupant delivered his upward heave.

Houdini always sprang into the can so energetically that the water overflowed, giving him an air space. Thus he could breathe while effecting his escape. But, sure as he was of success, Houdini always had his assistant Collins standing by with an ax, ready to hack open the milk can and release the water in case of an emergency.

In contrast, an escape artist named Genesta constructed a clever milk can with a thin triple wall, the middle sector working up and down with the smooth precision of a plunger, a device which utterly defied detection. One night, Genesta arrived in town late. He was just in time to set up the milk can and go on with the act. After he'd been locked in the milk can for five minutes, his assistants realized that an emergency had arisen.

Frantically, they pulled away the cabinet and tried to unlock the half-dozen padlocks that held the top in place. But the keys had gotten mixed and more precious minutes were lost in trying the locks. When the milk can finally was opened, Genesta was found drowned.

The very intricacy of the device had proven its fault. The milk can had been handled roughly while being loaded on a truck and its side had been dented. That wouldn't have mattered with any of Houdini's milk cans. With Genesta's, it caused the smooth-fitting plunger wall to lock with the others. The trick just refused to work. Genesta's props were auctioned off later and everything was sold except the milk can. It found no bidders.

Houdini never had a close call with his milk can, but his precautions paid off, years later, when Hardeen, as his successor, was working the escape at a wholesale liquor dealer convention. As a stunt, the milk can was filled with a popular brand of whisky, literally gallons of it, though much diluted. Despite that, when the lid was clamped, the fumes from the alcohol gathered in the air space with the effect of ether and Hardeen was completely overcome. But Collins was there with the fire ax and hacked the milk can open with time to spare.

It was because of his experience with various challenges that Houdini prepared for all possible emergencies. With a new escape, he never could tell what would happen until he tried it. Sometimes he deliberately accepted specified conditions that promised death with failure, his biggest thriller being an escape from the mouth of a loaded cannon which had a twenty-minute fuse set and ignited.

This happened in Chatham, England, on one of his periodic tours. The challenge was made by four petty officers of the Royal Navy, who specified that they would lash him to the muzzle of the cannon, using a rifle barrel to pin his arms behind his back, bringing his hands to his chest, where they were to be securely tied.

Actually, instead of making the escape harder, the rifle barrel was Houdini's insurance. He was lashed so tightly that he couldn't begin to get at his wrist knots, but he was able to work his arms and body laterally, always toward the same side. The escape was done in full view of several thousand persons who watched breathlessly while Houdini gradually inched the rifle barrel from beneath his arms.

It was a slow-motion race between the inching barrel and

the burning fuse. In twelve minutes, the end of the barrel passed Houdini's arm and an excited cry arose as he came half free. After that, it took him less than another minute to complete the release. But what Houdini most remembered was the warning that the Chatham police chief gave him before he started the escape.

The chief branded the escape as a foolish and dangerous stunt, not only to Houdini, but to the spectators. He declared that if anyone should be hurt, he would hold Houdini fully and solely responsible. He overlooked the fact that if something did go wrong, there wouldn't be anything left of Houdini on which to pin the blame.

In Germany, Houdini undertook a similar death race with the Berlin–Dresden Express. He allowed himself to be lashed to the railroad tracks a few miles outside of Dresden, exactly fifteen minutes before the swift train was due, picking a spot where the crowd could watch him from a hillside. Houdini had first tested this escape and was confident he could manage it in less than ten minutes. In fact, Houdini was running so far ahead of schedule, that he was planning to stall for time, when the express suddenly appeared around a bend.

Houdini had just freed his hands and was working to release his feet, which were tied to the other rail. He no longer had time to get them completely free, but as the train thundered closer, he managed to gain enough slack to throw his body over the far side of the track and pull his feet, still bound, down beside the rail. The wheels of the locomotive missed him by inches, and cut the ropes instead.

This happened on the side of the track away from the onlookers. After the express had roared by, they were looking for signs of Houdini's mangled body when, to their amazement, he arose from beyond the track and gave the ropes a triumphant toss.

Houdini's challenges included escapes from trunks, safes, barrels, coffins and whatever else people were willing to provide. Naturally, these fell into patterns. Trunks and safes, for example, were designed to keep people out, not in. With proper tools, they were quite vulnerable, though the audience regarded them as formidable. But here, again, an emergency might crop up with any previously untested case.

What was probably one of Houdini's closest calls and most certainly his luckiest escape occurred when he accepted a challenge to escape from a giant milk churn provided by the manufacturer. The churn was a huge contrivance, made of wood, with a flat top that clamped from the outside, but one look at it gave Houdini his big idea.

All he would need to get out of that churn was a thin metal wedge, which he could easily smuggle in with him. Houdini was sure he could force the edge under the flat top and thus get at the outside clamp, but it might take a lot of time and patience. Therefore, Houdini specified that air holes would have to be bored in the side of the churn, to which the challengers agreed.

Houdini gauged the number of holes by his packing-box escape, but once he was imprisoned in the churn, he found that his cramped body blocked most of the air holes and that he was rapidly running short of breath. By then, the cabinet had been lowered over the churn. Shouting would have done no good, for even if his voice had carried, which was unlikely, it would have been drowned by the orchestra which had begun to play a loud march, as it always did while an escape of this type was in progress.

It was impossible to do the wedge job with the few minutes that Houdini had left, and in desperation he began rocking the churn, hoping it would overturn and roll out through the front of the cabinet. Houdini's assistants, trained to accept the unexpected as an emergency, would then promptly open it. In that case, Houdini intended to have more air holes bored, so that he could resume the escape.

But for the moment, he was fighting for his life and not

worrying beyond that point. At last he managed to topple the churn. As he braced himself for the impact, he heard a peculiar clack, just as the churn top hit the floor. The top itself had fallen free, giving Houdini all the air he needed.

By luck, the churn had hit squarely on the clamp, knocking it open and automatically releasing Houdini. As he scrambled out, he made a mad effort to prevent the churn from rolling out through the front of the cabinet as he had previously planned. He succeeded in stopping it and promptly set it upright, clamping the top back in place.

Then he stepped out and took his bow, while the amazed committee that had brought the churn proceeded to examine it, wondering how he had possibly made his escape in so little time.

In 1907 Houdini was booked by the Keith circuit shortly before the theatrical chain of Klaw and Erlanger decided to invade the vaudeville field. Just as he had summoned Dash to Germany, Harry cabled him to come back to America from England and play the opposition. Klaw and Erlanger grabbed Hardeen as a headliner before he was off the boat. This time the competition lay between the theater circuits, so the brothers had to fake a grudge fight.

Houdini had started jumping from bridges while handcuffed, making his escape underwater, so Hardeen did the same. Houdini then decided to jump from superstructures to make the escape more sensational, and nearly came a cropper in Portland, Maine. There, he picked his bridge, checked the water's depth and advertised the jump, but when he arrived at the scheduled hour, the tide was out. That put a dozen feet more of jump into that much less water, but Houdini went ahead with it. Hardeen received the clippings and took a sixty-footer into the Ohio at Louisville.

In Detroit, Houdini did an early winter jump, came up underneath the ice, and had to find his way back to the hole that had been chopped to receive him. Hardeen made a midwinter jump at Norfolk, barely missing ice cakes that were floating past.

On the stage, each was escaping from packing cases, trunks, barrels, safes, or whatever the public wanted to bring there. When Houdini broke out of an antique witch's chair in Massachusetts, Hardeen did the same from a tramp chair in Maine.

The rivalry ended when the theatrical interests declared a truce, but the brothers were to fake their grudge fight again in 1915. By then, Houdini was performing perhaps the greatest of all his escapes, the "Chinese Water Torture Cell." This consisted of a large upright cabinet, glass-fronted and with metal bars inside, which was filled with water preparatory to the ordeal.

Houdini, in a bathing suit, had his ankles locked in a pair of stocks which formed the top of the cabinet. He was hoisted over the cell and hung there upside down while he drew long breaths and was finally lowered into the cabinet, where he was visible through the glass front.

The top was rapidly locked in place and a curtained cabinet placed over all. Through the corner of the curtain, looking in at the cell, peered Collins, Houdini's chief assistant, ready with an ax to crash the glass in case the escape failed. The metal bars would then have retained Houdini while the water escaped through the broken pane.

It never did fail during the actual performance, though there were some rehearsal accidents. The orchestra would howl away with "Sailor Beware." Then, within four minutes, the curtain would be flung aside and Houdini would appear dripping wet, waving for the cabinet to be hauled away so that the committee could inspect the cell and find it not only intact, but locked.

While baffling to the vast majority of onlookers, the working of the "Water Torture Cell" was fairly obvious to some escape artists, even though Houdini guarded its secret closely. This was proven immediately after Houdini first tried out the escape in Germany, in the fall of 1912. A rival act appeared with a girl called Miss Undina escaping from a similar cell. Houdini brought legal action and stopped the imitator, but it was apparent that some mechanical device was responsible for the escape, rather than the performer's skill.

Analyzed, the trick depended on the top, as that was the only route whereby a rapid exit could be made. The pair of stocks which formed the top were made of wood bound with strips of brass, and in one type, the rear section could be released after the stocks were locked, enabling it to slide from the brass binding, drawer-fashion. The joints at the rear corners were so neatly fitted that they defied detection during the preliminary examination.

Inside the cell, Houdini gripped the metal bars at the front and doubled himself upward until his head came above water inside the top, which was recessed to allow air. Then it was simply a case of releasing the rear section and sliding it backward from his ankles. This freed his legs, so that he could twist upright within the cell and clamber out through the opening. He then pushed the slide back in place and locked it. All this was done after the cell was covered by the cabinet, so there was no visible clue to the method.

In 1915, Houdini was booked on the Orpheum circuit in California, and the advance publicity on the "Water Torture Cell" was so tremendous that the competing Pantages circuit engaged Hardeen to present the "Milk Can Escape" as a rival attraction. In city after city the brothers appeared as opposition, and they frequently had their pictures taken alongside billboards advertising their acts.

The Orpheum circuit became worried by the competition; and when Houdini arrived in Oakland, the management insisted that he put on a special publicity stunt. So Houdini worked the strait-jacket escape while hanging upside down in full view of a vast crowd. Hardeen also specialized in the strait-jacket escape and he saw a chance to capitalize on it.

While Harry was struggling in the strait jacket at the top of a building far overhead, Dash sent boys through the crowd passing out show bills that read: "Hardeen—Now Playing at Pantages."

"It was the easiest outdoor stunt I ever did," Hardeen related afterward. "But was Harry burned up when he found out. It took him a couple of weeks to see the humor of it."

A few years later, Houdini performed the largest stage illusion in history, the "Vanishing Elephant," at the New York Hippodrome. The vanish required an enormous cabinet, with a narrowing interior, so that the audience could see through when the front was opened, even though the elephant was concealed at one side. Yet Houdini's great showmanship, along with the fact that the cabinet looked smaller than it was, made it a capital mystery that left the audience puzzled.

Soon after World War I, Houdini became a movie star and produced his own serial pictures. But he was eager to take out a full evening show, which he finally did in the fall of 1925. All that season and part of the next, audiences throughout the United States and Canada saw Houdini perform his magic in person, from small tricks to large, including his famous "Water Torture Cell," which was presented as a special act.

Houdini also introduced some classic effects, one being a crystal casket that had belonged to Robert-Houdin. Coins appeared magically inside the suspended casket, due to an ingenious mechanism that released them from a secret compartment in the decorated top. Another of Houdini's illusions was the original "Paligenisia." He had bought it from Dr. Lynn's son in England, and presented it exactly as when he had first seen it as a boy in Milwaukee. As the climax to his show, Houdini exposed the methods of fake spirit mediums, challenging them to produce their marvels on his stage, and offering to duplicate all their wonders by natural means. This created a sensation in many cities where Houdini played.

During the week of October 17, 1926, Houdini appeared in Montreal, and one morning toward the end of his engagement, a group of college students stopped at the theater to interview him. Houdini talked about the physical fitness needed in his escape acts, and demonstrated how he could brace the muscles of his abdomen to offset heavy blows. One student, then another, delivered punches at Houdini's invitation. As a third hesitated, Houdini relaxed, thinking the youth had given up the idea. Instead, the student made a belated swing. Houdini received the punch off guard, and it nearly crumpled him, but he managed to brush it off as if it had not hurt him.

That night, he complained of a pain in his side, which grew steadily worse. When the show reached Detroit, he was running a fever, but still insisted upon giving his performance when he learned that the theater was sold out. That was Houdini's last show. He collapsed at the finish and was rushed to a hospital, suffering from an acute case of appendicitis. Surgeons operated immediately, but peritonitis was so far advanced that they were unable to save the patient's life. He died on Halloween, 1926.

Houdini willed his show to Hardeen, who continued to perform many of Houdini's famous tricks and illusions for nearly twenty years. For several seasons, Hardeen worked Houdini's "Overboard Box Escape" at Atlantic City. This was similar to the "Packing Box Escape," but instead of being placed in a cabinet, the box was weighted and dropped off the end of a pier, where Hardeen made his escape beneath the surface of the ocean.

In June, 1945, Hardeen, then sixty-nine years old, gave his last vaudeville performance, finishing with the "Milk Can Escape," which he still presented in his inimitable style. That same month, he died following a brief illness. More than half a century had passed since Ehrich and Theo Weiss made their debut as the Houdini Brothers. Now, both were gone. The epoch of the escape kings was closed.

Chapter 8

The Great Raymond

(1877–1948)

Addison the Magician had a problem that all his sorcery could not solve. In the summer of 1886, he was ready to start a tour from his home in Ohio to the Pacific Coast and back, when he learned that the youth who served as his assistant had been stricken with typhoid fever and could not go along.

There wasn't time to train a new helper, and the situation seemed hopeless until Addison thought of his nephew, Raymond Saunders. Although Raymond was only nine years old, he was a bright boy, and he had watched his uncle rehearse the show so often that he knew exactly what the assistant was supposed to do.

Addison talked it over with Raymond's father, who decided to let the boy go along, as he would be back by the time school opened in the fall. Naturally, young Raymond was enthusiastic when they told him, and soon he was off on a three months' trip with Uncle Addison.

Most of the engagements were for one night only, which made it very tiring for Addison. But to his nephew Raymond, the tour was a thrill from start to finish. It had been one thing to watch his uncle rehearse his act until the tricks seemed old and tiresome. It was another matter to be up on the stage with the magician, witnessing the awe of the spectators who regarded each marvel as something new and in-

186

credible. Long before those one-night stands were over, Raymond had contracted a fever quite different from that of the assistant he had replaced. Raymond's was the magic fever.

When they returned home, Addison went into the photographic business and packed away his magical equipment. But Raymond was hooked. He practiced both magic and juggling on his own, and after a few years he persuaded his uncle to give him the discarded apparatus. Once he had acquired that, Raymond, then fourteen years old, joined a circus with his magic act, staying with it so long that his family had a hard time finding him and bringing him home.

Addison tried to smooth the situation by taking Raymond to see Herrmann the Great. After the show they went backstage to meet the master magician, but instead of being awed by Herrmann's presence, Raymond's ambition was fired all the more. All he could talk about was how, some day, he would travel everywhere as the Great Raymond, a true disciple of Herrmann.

Since travel seemed the proper antidote for Raymond's mania for magic, his grandfather, who was going on a business trip to Europe, decided to take him along. The prospect delighted young Raymond, as it enabled him to meet more people to whom he could show his favorite tricks. In London, he so amazed his grandfather's friends that they arranged for him to present a series of programs as a "boy magician." The highlight was his appearance at a lawn fete held by Queen Victoria.

That was Raymond's first command performance and it led to another before the Prince of Wales, who later became Edward VII. Among those present was Charles Bertram, one of the most accomplished of English magicians, who finished all his tricks with the catch phrase, "Isn't it wonderful!" Bertram was a great friend of the Prince, whom he had tutored in sleight of hand. When Raymond saw that the two were seated together, he could not resist the temptation to impress them both.

In beginning some card tricks, Raymond bent the pack and sprang the cards from one hand to the other, a customary procedure among magicians. Knowing that Bertram was a master card manipulator, who could spring the pack with his hands an arm's length apart, Raymond intended to display the same skill.

However, in springing the cards, Raymond overdid it. He lost control of a dozen cards, which scattered over the floor, leaving him in an utter dilemma. He would have to pick up the cards and start over or lay the rest of the pack aside, and either course would be an admission of an ignominious failure.

While Raymond stood frozen in consternation, Bertram arose from his chair, stooped and gathered up the fallen cards. He spread the cards between his hands, showing them to everyone including his royal patron. Then, raising his eyebrows in a manner of real surprise, Bertram remarked: "Why, I was positive that these cards were all strung together, but none of them are! Isn't it wonderful?"

With that, he handed the stray cards to Raymond, gave a bow of admiration, and gestured for him to go on. Raymond caught an approving nod from the Prince of Wales, who was also "in the know." Soon, Raymond was springing the pack perfectly while he acknowledged Bertram's courtesy with a grateful smile.

Raymond met Bertram a few times later and learned much from their brief friendship. Though essentially a sleight-of-hand performer, Bertram did colorful tricks with hats, handkerchiefs and livestock, so he could put on a very lavish program with comparatively few props. By introducing two or three stage illusions, he would have as big a show as any occasion might demand.

This came as a revelation to young Raymond. After seeing Herrmann's show, he had thought of featuring big illusions and filling in with smaller effects. Even more pointed was Bertram's final advice; that was to avoid using stage traps when presenting illusions. When Raymond asked why, Bertram told him.

Once, Bertram had been performing in a small hall, where his finale was the magical production of a huge flag, which he spread wide with both arms as he stepped back to take a bow. Behind him was a stage trap, and as he put his considerable weight on it, he learned that it had a weak bolt underneath, for a moment later, he landed in the cellar.

Bertram added that he managed to come upstairs and step on from the wing to take a bow. He found that the audience was quite as dazed as he was. The big flag had fluttered down to the stage and had covered the trap, so that no one had any idea where he had gone. They all agreed that the trick was a real "stunner," and Bertram subscribed to that same sentiment. But he never wanted to try it again.

After returning back home to Ohio, Raymond finished school and began to study medicine at Western Reserve University. He might have given up his magic entirely, when hypnotism, which had gained medical recognition in 1892, suddenly created a nationwide furore. Professional hypnotists were springing up everywhere, and Raymond, as a medical student, was better qualified than most to enter the new field.

His knowledge of magic enabled him to detect the tricks that many self-styled hypnotists were using to bluff the public, and by 1896, Raymond was putting on magic shows with hypnotism as the main feature. He tried to work his performances in between college terms and during vacations, but he finally reached the point where he had to give up one or the other, medicine or magic.

Magic won when Raymond's performances attracted the attention of Major James B. Pond, a well-known producer in the entertainment field, who had booked the route for Addison ten years before. Pond had brought European mind readers and Oriental mystics to the United States; now, when he learned that Raymond was familiar with those subjects and versed in hypnotism and the tricks of fake mediums as well, he saw a great opportunity for the display of such talents abroad.

Almost anything seemed possible in that period of amazing expansion. Railways and telegraph lines were spreading everywhere and great steamships plied the oceans between continents linked by undersea cables. Shows could be booked anywhere within a few days, and engagements fulfilled within a matter of weeks, or a few months at most.

The world was an oyster for anyone willing to pry it wide, and young Raymond, though not yet twenty-one, was eager to have a try. Major Pond won over the family, so Raymond packed the best of his equipment—including some of Addison's old props—and with his father as his business manager, started out on his first world tour.

Shows, lectures and demonstrations were arranged in advance, and others were scheduled by cable while en route. Hong Kong, Calcutta, Bombay, Ceylon, were all magic names to Raymond when he started his tour, but they proved responsive to *his* magic as well. While he traveled, he concentrated on learning the languages of the countries in which he appeared, and quickly picked up enough to comment on the keynotes of his tricks.

On ship as well as shore, Raymond's magic was in great demand, and often he booked shows in return for passage. It was on one such voyage that he met Mark Twain, who was making a year's lecture tour around the world. The humorist's tour had been arranged by Major Pond, and Raymond introduced himself as a friend of the Major. Mark Twain then declared that he would personally introduce the Great Raymond to the ship's passengers when he presented his show. That evening, as the liner glided through a calm tropical sea, Mark Twain arose before the assembled throng, gestured to the smiling young man who stood beside a velvet-draped table holding a wand in his hand, and spoke in his most serious tone.

The ship's passengers were most fortunate, Mark Twain said, to have with them that evening the Great Raymond, a true master of mystery and more. He had remarkable qualities which Mark Twain was sure that the company would soon discern; and he went on to describe Raymond as handsome, clever and gifted with a wonderful personality. They would find that every word that Raymond uttered literally sparkled with humor and wit.

There, Mark Twain paused, while Raymond, overwhelmed by the introduction, swelled with pride. And, then:

"In short," summed Mark Twain, "he is the Mark Twain of Magic."

That really rocked the boat. Mark Twain had stolen the show before it began. During his act, Raymond heard laughs where the audience usually gave mere chuckles and he realized that they were comparing him to Mark Twain. It proved the value of a clever quip, and Raymond put it to immediate profit by adding witty comments in every show he gave. He later made the most of the endorsement by billing himself as "the Mark Twain of Magic."

Though Raymond's first world tour was profitable, it ended abruptly in Buenos Aires, where he arrived during 1898 in response to urgent cables offering him six months of engagements in the Argentine Republic. By that time, the Spanish-American War had broken out, and since sentiment in the Argentine was pro-Spanish, Raymond headed home to the United States.

There, escape acts were the rage, so Raymond joined the ranks of "handcuff kings," shaking off shackles on the stage and breaking out of local jails. He had worked escapes before, and he continued to accept handcuff and jail challenges throughout his career, wherever they were in demand. But, like hypnotism,

Raymond regarded escape work simply as a secondary phase of his over-all presentation of magic and mystery.

Raymond's mind-reading feats were equally sensational. In one, he blindfolded himself, then drove a team of horses through the main street of a town to find an object hidden by a committee in some obscure place. Such demonstrations brought people to the theaters in droves to witness Raymond's remarkable mind-reading performance on the stage. Almost from the start, Raymond had duplicated feats of fake spirit mediums, and he gradually developed those tricks into an entire act, which he called "A Trip to Spookville."

Raymond also presented his version of the great trunk mystery, which he styled "The Flight of Satteka." A girl was handcuffed, then put inside a sack, which was sealed and placed in a trunk. The trunk was both examined and locked by a committee, a cabinet was set over it, and with a whisk of the front curtain, Raymond instantly changed places with the girl.

Another of Raymond's larger mysteries was the "Phantom Supper," known in magicians' parlance as the "Organ Pipes." In this intriguing effect, the curtain rose showing two trestles supporting a thin board or sheet of glass. Upon it were half a dozen cylinders set in a row and numbered from 1 to 6. Each was about sixteen inches tall, but they decreased slightly in diameter from six inches downward, thus resembling organ pipes. Raymond stated that they were all he managed to save from a shipwreck, but through his wizardry, he had been able to put them to good use where the survivors were concerned.

With that, he showed the pipes empty, one by one. To prove the absence of any trickery, he dropped each pipe through the one before; number 2 through number 1; number 3 through number 2; and so on, showing each new pipe empty immediately afterward. When he came to the final pipe, he thrust his arm clear through.

Then, with the pipes lined up in their original positions,

Raymond invited his assistants to be seated on chairs beside a bare table, and proceeded to provide them with a magical banquet. From one pipe, he produced a large cloth which he spread on the table. He followed that by bringing knives, forks, plates and glasses from another cylinder. Continuing along the line, he produced napkins, a loaf of bread, a roast chicken, sausages, vegetables and bottles of wine from which he filled the glasses. Finally Raymond brought from a pipe a vase with a bunch of flowers to complete the table setting for the incredible repast, which seemed so large that the pipes could hardly have held it! But the big question was how anything could be produced from cylinders that were so obviously empty.

Actually, the extreme measures taken to show the pipes empty was the real key to the secret. Five of the cylinders— all except the largest, number 1—were loaded at the start. The contents were packed in loose-fitting inner tubes, each with a flat hook extending up over the upper edge of the numbered pipe. Most of the contents were compressible, and others were nested, like the glasses and the bottles. The latter were merely shells, except one from which wine was poured. In fact, shell bottles were sometimes used for the inner tubes that held the loads.

After showing the audience that pipe number 1 was empty, Raymond "proved" his point by dropping pipe number 2 down through it, as already described. The hook projecting from number 2 automatically engaged the upper edge of pipe number 1, transferring the load to the latter. Since number 1 had already been shown empty, Raymond simply set it down and let the audience look through pipe number 2, which was now empty.

Similarly, he transferred the load from number 3 to number 2; from number 4 to number 3; and so on, showing each to be empty. Raymond then produced the contents of the cylinders, beginning with the tablecloth and following with the rest in

a well-rehearsed order. From number 5, he brought a large napkin which had a compressible load in its folds. In spreading the
napkin, he carried it above number 6 and let the extra load
drop there, so articles could later be produced from pipe number 6.

As if all this were not enough, Raymond carried a full evening program of smaller magic, specializing in close-up tricks,
which he presented in his own deft, humorous style. He produced hundreds of silk handkerchiefs and flags, cooked cakes
in borrowed hats, filled the stage with flowers that appeared
from empty baskets, and brought a whole barnyard of rabbits,
ducks, pigeons and chickens from equally empty boxes.

Raymond's program was so diversified that he could switch
to any form of mystification; handcuffs, mind reading, hypnotism or straight magic. He could also double by playing two
parts on a vaudeville program, and he could divide a full evening magic show into three distinct acts.

By the end of six years, Raymond had toured the entire
United States and had assembled his own company, all special-
ists in some branch of entertainment—music, acrobatics, dancing or comedy—enabling him to take the big gamble he had
been planning all along. That was to embark on another world
tour with the biggest magic show ever assembled for that purpose.

When Raymond broke the news, the whole company agreed
to go along. Their first stop was Cuba, which had calmed down
after the revolt of 1906. Business proved tremendous, and the
newspapers ran cartoons depicting Raymond's magic settling
the political problems of the island republic. From there the
show traveled through the West Indies to the Guianas, then
Brazil, and finally reached the Argentine.

During those last few years in the United States, Raymond,
already an accomplished linguist from his first world tour, had
been learning the languages of the countries where he planned
to appear. He spoke Spanish in Cuba, French in Martinique,

Dutch in Surinam, Portuguese in Rio de Janeiro, and Spanish again in Buenos Aires, along with smatterings of German and Italian for the benefit of persons of such nationalities who had settled in the Argentine.

That won audiences as nothing else could, not even Raymond's magic. At first, his discourse was simply a translation of the English that he used with his tricks, but when the audience called back comments, he was quick to catch their meaning and answer them with suitable quips in the local vernacular, just as he had in different sections of the United States. To Raymond, it was all a game that became more intriguing, the longer he played it.

Raymond had hoped to stay at least six months in South America; instead, he remained there almost three years. He had indeed shown foresight in so thoroughly equipping himself with both magic and talent, for he was frequently called upon to play return engagements, which meant changing the major portion of his program. He was also able to travel light when taking side trips to remote towns where it was too costly or too difficult to carry the whole show.

However, Raymond had much of his equipment with him on a trip up the coast of Brazil when the steamer on which his show was traveling struck a submerged derelict and sank so rapidly that there was no chance to save any of the baggage. Raymond and the dozen members of his company drifted on a life raft for three days, subsisting on hardtack. They did not even have the magic "organ pipes" to provide themselves with a "phantom feast," for those had gone down with the show.

A rising storm was carrying them still farther out to sea when they were sighted by a fishing trawler. The vessel took them aboard and brought them into an obscure port. There the troupe was stranded, for most of Raymond's funds had gone into steamship tickets, leaving them no money for living expenses or transportation, and no show to put on, if they did get anywhere.

Into that dismal picture stepped a wealthy local planter who had heard of Raymond's show and was anxious to see it. He immediately provided for the troupe's living expenses; then, with a wave of his hand, he told Raymond to build all the tricks he wanted and to cable anywhere for whatever special equipment he required. The planter took care of all the bills, and within a month, the Raymond company was able to put on a full evening show for their Brazilian benefactor.

By the time the tour was ended, Raymond had paid back all the money the Brazilian had advanced, for business was good throughout South America. When disaster struck again, it furnished a fantastic reverse twist that proved to be to Raymond's advantage.

During the tour, Raymond had been featuring the jail escape under the same rigid conditions as in the United States. He allowed himself to be stripped, searched, then shackled and manacled in a jail cell which was locked from the outside. Yet after the police chief had retired to his office along with the committee, Raymond invariably arrived there in a matter of minutes, entirely free!

The escape depended on a knowledge of handcuffs and locks, a supply of keys and picks, and clever ways of planting the needed implements in the cell without the committee knowing it. The fewer keys required, the easier it was to hide them in the cell, so whenever possible, Raymond checked the cuffs and locks beforehand and prepared accordingly. There were fewer makes of cuffs in South America, which was helpful, but there was always the chance of encountering some peculiar pattern or an unusual lock.

That meant making a special packet of keys for the occasion, as was the case in the Argentine city of Mendoza, where Raymond accepted a jailbreak challenge. The police were very polite; they let him try the cuffs they intended to use, and he was allowed to look over the cell a few times. At the scheduled time, Raymond was handcuffed, manacled and locked in the cell, while his clothes were locked in another cell farther down the corridor.

Fifteen minutes was the time allotted for the handcuff king to get out of the first cell, unlock the other cell, put on his clothes and reach the police chief's office, though the chief, in departing, said he would extend the time to a half hour if needed.

Raymond was amused at that, for he figured the whole job wouldn't take five minutes. When the outer door clanged, he obtained the hidden keys, only to find that they wouldn't work. He had planted the wrong packet in the cell!

Through the barred window, Raymond looked across the plaza to his hotel. He saw the window of his room, and even pictured the desk drawer where the needed keys must be. But his only hope was to struggle with those he had right now. Struggle he did, but none of the keys would do. People were arriving in the plaza, eager to be on hand when the escape king emerged from the jail. Fifteen minutes passed—then twenty— and the crowd had reached a feverish pitch that Raymond more than matched, for he hadn't managed to slip loose from a single cuff.

Raymond's escape would be big news; but his failure would be bigger. Only it chanced that something still bigger was due. Just before the half hour ended, when Raymond was really about to give up, he heard an approaching rumble. The window bars quivered; across the way, the hotel seemed to wobble as people scattered wildly. Then the cell itself was shaking; its front wall crumbled away.

The town had been hit by an earthquake. Tremors were common in the area, but this was heavier than usual. Years before, Mendoza had been leveled by a quake, so now the buildings were of light construction, the jail included. The fallen wall formed a rough slope from the cell down to the deserted plaza and Raymond gingerly made a descent amid the rubble.

Next, he was hobbling across the plaza, clad only in locked chains and handcuffs, the most astonishing sight in all Mendoza. But no one had stayed to witness his bizarre journey.

Raymond reached the hotel and found the empty lobby strewn with plaster. He went up the tilted stairs to his room, located the right keys, unlocked the cuffs and put on spare clothes. When the tremors ended, he left the hotel and went back to the jail to announce his escape and return the handcuffs to the police chief.

In Brazil, another singular coincidence provided Raymond with the idea for one of his greatest tricks. He was in a museum chatting with some naturalists who had brought back many remarkable butterflies from the Amazon region, and he was studying the magnificent specimens that adorned the walls when he noticed a butterfly net that belonged to one of the professors.

The net was so much larger and the handle so much longer than usual, that Raymond asked to try it. He gave it a wide, high sweep and instantly a pair of wings spread within the net, as though a phantom bird had arrived there. Still more amazing, when Raymond finished his swoop, the thing was gone. The speechless professors were sure that they were watching some of Raymond's magic, until they realized that he was quite as astonished as they were.

Another swing of the net and the mysterious bird appeared again, only to vanish as it had before. Even when they looked into the net closely, none of the men could trace the phantom until they used a strong light and jiggled the net slightly. Then, a quiver of wings provided the answer.

A huge night moth had flown into the net, remaining there unnoticed, as it was long and thin, like a knife edge, until it spread its wings when swung into the light. When the moth folded its wings again, it dwindled back to almost nothing. The sight was so surprising that Raymond decided to put it to practical use.

Back at the theater, he rigged a large fish net with a pair of spreading rods to which feathers were attached. Actuated from the handle, these resembled bird wings when the net was swung in air. As the net dipped to a metal basket, the wings were folded in again, but at the same instant, a live pigeon was released as though delivered from the net.

The illusion was perfect and soon Raymond was netting bird after bird from mid-air. The fame of the "Pigeon Catching" spread, and like all such novelties, it eventually became a standard item in the programs of many magicians.

In 1909 the Great Raymond arrived in London and appeared at the Hackney Empire Theatre, where he created an immense sensation with his comedy spirit séance "A Trip to Spookville," which was seen in England for the first time. He first set an artificial hand on a square of glass, and the hand mysteriously tapped responses to any questions put to it. Raymond was then tied hand and foot and placed under a canopy with some tambourines, which immediately began to strum and bang; yet when the curtain was lifted, he was still tightly bound. Next, a man from the audience joined him under the canopy, more commotion followed and the volunteer was found with his coat and vest off, a bucket on his head and bells around his neck, all seemingly the work of gamboling ghosts.

While in London, Raymond gave a command performance for King Edward VII, who was still intrigued by conjuring, though his friend Bertram had died a few years before. In one mind-reading trick, Raymond used a pack of cards which he had previously set or "stacked" in a special order. He gave the cards a skillful false shuffle that looked genuine enough, but did not disturb the arrangement.

Imagine Raymond's concern when his Majesty asked politely, "May I shuffle that pack?" There was nothing to do but hand over the cards and think of some other trick to replace the one that was being ruined. When King Edward finished his thorough shuffle, Raymond received the pack, fanned it and gave the cards a passing glance while still considering what to do.

A moment later, Raymond was proceeding with the original trick, for, to his amazement, he had noted that the cards were still in their exact order!

Now he recalled that Bertram had instructed King Edward in sleight of hand. The king, recognizing that Raymond was using a prearranged pack, had purposely asked for the cards to supply a perfect false shuffle of his own, making the trick all the more wonderful.

In sharp contrast was Raymond's performance for Kaiser Wilhelm II, of Germany, on his private yacht, the *Hohenzollern*. The kaiser covered his interest with a gloss of disdain and would not even touch the pack that Raymond proffered, but motioned for one of his attendants to take a card instead.

Raymond toured the British Isles to capacity business, changing his show and increasing its size. He set up a complete workshop in London for the construction of new illusions, and eventually he had enough for six complete shows. Then he toured the entire continent of Europe, where the variety and excellence of his show, and his familiarity with the languages in all the countries that he visited, won him acclaim that no other magician had ever achieved.

In those years prior to the First World War, when royalty flourished throughout Europe, Raymond deservedly gained the dual title of the "King of Magicians and the Magician of Kings." The monarchs of Portugal, Spain, Belgium, Holland, Italy, Austria and Russia all witnessed his magic from their royal boxes or through the prerogative of command performances. Many entertainers would have pressed that advantage to the limit, but not Raymond.

Instead of seeking repeat engagements, he started eastward on another world tour, leaving European royalty to wait until he circled the globe and came back more famous then ever. His was a precarious fame that needed further achievements to support it. Little did he realize that the rulers of Europe were dwelling in fanciful castles constructed of tinsel flimsier than his own.

When Raymond reached India in 1912, he was carrying forty tons of paraphernalia valued at fifty thousand dollars, enough for four full-evening shows. Immense colored posters depicting varied mysteries and illusions were plastered over building walls in every city where Raymond appeared.

His show featured the biggest "Noah's Ark" illusion ever built. When set up, it dominated the stage and became practically an act in itself. Opened wide, the ark was shown convincingly empty from all angles; when closed, it disgorged doves, chickens, ducks, rabbits, cats and dogs as in the earlier versions. These, however, were followed by geese, monkeys, sheep, goats and other sizable animals. For a climax, two girls emerged from the mysterious ark.

As the tour proceeded, new and unusual creatures were added to the magical menagerie: parrots, macaws, cockatoos, a cheetah and a dwarf deer. Eventually both an anteater and an armadillo joined the bizarre crew. Raymond often quipped that if he were again shipwrecked, he would bring his company to shore in his own ark, animals and all, which was why he took it on his world tour.

Actually, Raymond had chosen all his illusions on the strength of their appeal to foreign audiences. His knowledge of Oriental psychology, gained on his first world tour, enabled him to present mysteries that were not only new to their viewers, but captured their full interest. In India, Raymond gave many performances for rulers of native states; later, he appeared before the King of Siam and the Mikado of Japan.

While touring India, Raymond frequently witnessed the work of fakirs, and gained a firsthand knowledge of their methods. For two years he posted a reward of one thousand pounds, then the equivalent of five thousand dollars, for anyone who could baffle him with the famous "Indian Rope Trick," in which the magician supposedly throws a rope straight up in the air, where it remains as rigid as a column while a boy climbs it and disappears. In some descriptions of the trick, the fakir also climbs the rope, carrying a huge sword. He, too, vanishes and the severed portions of the boy's body come tumbling down from the void. The fakir then reappears at the top of the rope, descends to the ground and restores the boy to life.

Many American and European magicians who visited India failed to find even a trace of the "Rope Trick." But Raymond, perhaps by dint of the large reward, claimed to have witnessed a well-faked version of the mystery, with some of its more fanciful embellishments. Instead of being taken to a remote valley in the Himalayas, where, according to reports, the "Rope Trick" was usually shown, he was conducted to a narrow courtyard flanked by buildings several stories in height, near the center of Calcutta.

Smudge fires filled the court with thick smoke that made people's eyes water and obscured everything above the second floor. The end of a coiled rope was thrown upward and remained suspended, hidden in the smoke. The reason was that a bamboo pole had been thrust across the court between third-story windows, and a lightweight native was perched there, unseen. He caught the rope, fastened it, and rapidly squirmed back to a window.

Next, a boy climbed the rope and seemingly vanished in the smoke. The fakir did not climb after him but simply tossed a sword straight up, so the boy could catch it. Soon, fake portions of a severed, bloodstained body came tumbling down from the thick smoke. These, of course, had been passed along to the boy by the confederate at the window.

Instead of restoring the boy, the fakir simply had helpers bundle away the fake body, while he pointed up to the smoke, from which the boy suddenly appeared and slid down the rope unharmed. Later, the rope itself dropped, and by the time the smoke cleared sufficiently to see the roofs of the buildings, the pole had been pulled away.

Of the more commonly performed feats of Hindu magic, Raymond classed two as outstanding: the "Basket Trick" and the "Mango Tree." In the "Basket Trick," a boy entered the mouth of an oval-shaped basket and the fakir covered him with a cloth. Suddenly the cloth collapsed, and the fakir trampled it down, even squatting in the basket to prove that the boy had totally vanished.

To convince the skeptics further, the fakir then ran the blade of a sword through the basket at all angles; after that, he drew out the cloth and spread it over the opening. All at once it rose upward and was whipped aside, revealing the boy standing there, back from his trip to nowhere.

Actually, the boy, who was a contortionist, coiled himself around inside the bulging side of the basket, which was more commodious than it appeared, allowing plenty of space for the fakir to squat in the center. The fakir's sword thrusts were carefully made at key spots, so the blade passed under the boy's arms, between his legs, or past his neck without harming him.

Oddly, in some cases, blood poured from holes in the basket when the fakir made his sword stabs, indicating that the boy was still there. Later, when brought from the basket, he proved uninjured. In this version, the boy carried a bladder filled with bullock's blood, and he squirted it through the sides of the basket following the sword thrusts. Raymond felt that the use of sword thrusts to prove the basket empty was made somewhat less convincing by the blood routine, but he noted that the onlookers were awed by either version and seemed to enjoy the gruesome effect of all the gore.

In the "Mango Tree," the fakir had pliant branches of various sizes wrapped around his body or concealed beneath cloths that were scattered on the ground beside him. He used one large cloth to form a little tent on a tripod of three sticks, and in planting a mango seed beneath the tent, he introduced the smallest of the branches.

After due claptrap, the tent was opened to show that the seed had sprouted, and a larger branch was secretly introduced while the tent was drawn shut again. This continued in successive stages, the climax being the disclosure of a three-foot tree, which was actually a branch with a few ripe mangoes that had been doubled up beforehand and was opened beneath the tent. But many tourists, after witnessing the trick, went home with exaggerated accounts of an eight-foot mango tree that had grown to full bloom before their very eyes.

In discussing Oriental magic, Raymond often stated that although Indian magic was simple, Japanese magic was still simpler. As examples, he cited two rituals he witnessed at Shinto celebrations of that era, the *Yubana*, or boiling water ordeal, and the *Hiwatari*, or fire walk.

In the *Yubana*, the performer approached a huge caldron filled with boiling water and suddenly thrust two clumps of bamboo twigs into the liquid, flinging it high and showering it all about his head, shoulders and arms. As the water reached the fire below the caldron, it produced great clouds of steam, which subsided only when the caldron was almost empty. The performer was then seen quite unharmed by the ordeal, proving the mighty power of Shinto.

Miraculous though this seemed to the average observer, the secret was quite simple. The *Yubana* ritual was timed to start soon after the water began to boil. This meant that although it was boiling at the surface, the water near the bottom of the caldron was still comparatively cool. Flaying the water simply mixed it, reducing the over-all temperature below the boiling point, and the showering further decreased its heat. The rising steam merely added to the effect.

In the *Hiwatari*, the Shintoists performed a ritual about a bed of flaming charcoal some nine feet long and four feet wide. The fire was raked with iron rods to form a mass of glowing coals, so hot that the spectators were forced to draw back from the sides. Despite that, each of the performers blandly walked barefooted through the searing furnace without experiencing the slightest harm.

In contrast to the water ordeal, the fire walk depended on delay. The fire was raked more heavily in the center, making it thinner there. Consequently its coals would begin to burn out while those at the sides were still red-hot. Often, salt was thrown over the fire as part of the ritual; most of it was tossed on the center to damp it even more.

By keeping strictly to the center, the fire-walkers trod on coals that were burnt out on the surface, and by walking steadily but without any lingering or hesitation, their feet did not remain on one spot long enough to contact the live coals beneath. Treading down the center path made it easier for those who followed the leader, and what helped "give away" the *Hiwatari* was the fact that bystanders were often invited to join the procession to prove that the powers of Shinto could be extended to protect them, too. Raymond, of course, was prompt to accept the invitation, and he closely observed the fiery trail from the moment he began his march.

Though the magic of the Far East offered little that the Great Raymond could add to his repertoire, he acquired many magnificent stage settings and other trappings, so that when he reached the United States by way of Manila and Honolulu, his show was the most elegant magical presentation that had ever been seen on the American stage. But it was the wonders of his wizardry, his fine appearance and his flawless execution that gained him deserved acclaim in his homeland.

Elbert Hubbard, the noted inspirational philosopher who wrote "A Message to Garcia," witnessed Raymond's performances, met him personally, heard of his adventures and was so impressed that he summed up his opinions in an article that ran in part:

When Daniel Webster landed on the dock at Liverpool, the stevedores pointed him out and said, "There goes the King of America." Daniel Webster looked the part; he had the solemn, impressive dignity of a man who knows the secrets of the Gods and scorns to pay his grocer. America does not especially need a king, but if I were to choose a man to jerk the scepter over us eight hours a day, I would name The Great Raymond.

Here is a man who has circled the globe in his professional capacity of instructing, astonishing and making the nations laugh. Raymond has played before more crowned heads than any other man living . . . and has tumbled all of them off their cosmic perches in catalyptic howls of laughter. . . . His conversation dazzles, sparkles, electrifies. He is wise, witty, subtle, keen, and has a vocabulary like a circus ad-writer. . . .

Every trick of every magician who ever lived is known to Raymond. He uses them all and goes them one better. . . . In Egypt, China, Japan and India, the very homes of illusion, Raymond makes his greatest successes. . . . The grace, the intelligence, the wit, the nimbleness and the skill of the man form the crowning result of twenty-five years of unremitting energy, concentration and practice. . . .

If we would make Raymond King of America, and send him round the world as a sample of our goods, just to advertise the United States of America, he would outstrip any lion-hunter who ever used smokeless powder. Raymond has the athletic body, the beaming eyes, the gracious, well-modulated voice, the hands that talk, the brain that thinks, the will that reinforces, all flavored by love into a consummate whole.

Great is "The Great Raymond."

That preachment by Fra Elbertus, as Elbert Hubbard termed himself, appeared in his magazine, *The Philistine*, in September,

1913. Six months later, Raymond had finished his engagements in the United States and was off on another world tour. He traveled southward through the Caribbean to Panama, then down the west coast of South America to Peru.

In Lima, Raymond's fluent command of the Spanish language and the magnificence of his new show brought capacity crowds to the Municipal Theater. As one critic put it, Raymond was a past master of all the Black Arts, whose personal charm and skill won the applause of *palco, butaca* and *galería* alike, and whose miracles were reminiscent of Grimm, Aesop and the Arabian Nights. Raymond also gave a special performance at the presidential palace, and it proved such a hit that it became the cover theme of a Peruvian magazine.

Audiences in other South American countries proved equally enthusiastic and Raymond spent a full two years playing through Chile, Argentina, Uruguay and Brazil. By then, the First World War had broken out. When the *Lusitania* was torpedoed, Raymond's friend Elbert Hubbard was among the victims. Yet despite the menace of U-boats, Raymond later took his show into the war zone. Beginning in August, 1916, he played an extended engagement in Paris; later he went to England, where he was performing when the war ended.

Shortly after World War I, Raymond began building a new show for another world tour. Meanwhile, he played theaters in London where business was excellent during the postwar period. There he tried out many new mysteries, among them the "Coffin Escape" that he had brought from South America. Raymond was placed in an examined coffin, the lid was put on and screwed down tight, but he quickly escaped from the somber contrivance once it had been placed out of sight beneath a canopy.

Raymond invited some fellow-magicians to see the "Coffin Escape" at a suburban theater near London. Box seats were reserved for the group, which included Will Goldston, a solemn, middle-aged London magic dealer who dressed conservatively and affected a degree of self-importance.

When Raymond let a local committee examine the coffin, they claimed it was different from any they had ever seen, and they argued that it wasn't genuine. Even though they couldn't discover the secret, which depended on a cleverly hidden catch at one end, Raymond was in a jam, because he had advertised that a standard coffin would be used. One beefy committeeman declared that if the coffin was a real one, they had a right to know where Raymond had gotten it.

Raymond blandly replied that the coffin had been supplied by a very reputable firm in London's West End. After a moment of pretended reflection, he even added the name: Jones and Howard, Limited, Casket Makers. The beefy spokesman snapped back that he had never heard of them. With a polite smile, Raymond informed the committee that Jones and Howard had sent along their own man to answer any questions, so they might just as well ask him.

He gestured toward the box where the magicians were seated and Will Goldston started looking around for the representative from Jones and Howard, only to realize that he was the person Raymond had indicated! A few moments later, Goldston was on his feet, hemming and hawing as he made up facts about a firm of coffin manufacturers that didn't exist. Raymond prompted him with a few reminders and soon the committee was convinced that "Jones and Howard" had insisted on supplying this new and somewhat odd-looking casket as a sample of the "coming thing" in funeral equipment, rather than the more conventional coffin that Raymond had ordered and would have preferred. That settled, Raymond proceeded with his escape, to the tumultuous acclaim of the audience.

In the fall of 1920, business on the continent having returned to normal, Raymond began a European tour, making frequent jumps from Amsterdam, Brussels and Paris back to London, where he kept a full-time workshop building new equipment and illusions. By 1924 he had tons of equipment in London warehouses and was ready to embark on an extended tour with a show more lavish than ever before. To add still greater variety, he again engaged specialty acts, which were interspersed with his magic. Raymond began his tour in England, and the show proved so successful that he continued for two years in Great Britain alone before playing the continent.

There, in one Spanish town, Raymond finished a matinee and went to a bullfight with the local chief of police. During the bullfight, someone brought the chief a message. After he read it, the police chief turned to Raymond and declared solemnly that he would have to arrest him. Raymond's advertising had stated that he would perform an escape act at that day's matinee, but he had failed to do so. It therefore became the chief's duty to take the magician back to face his accusers.

The audience was still at the theater when they arrived there and Raymond explained in his best Castilian that there had been a mistake in the billing. But the crowd still demanded his arrest for misrepresenting the show, so the police chief clamped a pair of handcuffs on Raymond's wrists and told him to come along to jail. Instead, Raymond wrenched away, whirled to the center of the stage and came about completely free of the handcuffs, which he returned, still locked, to the astonished police chief.

The rapid escape brought such enthusiasm from the audience that the chief decided Raymond had fulfilled the advertised terms. That announcement was received with unanimous approval and the police chief took the magician back to see the bullfight.

The "Coffin Escape" became so popular in Spain that Raymond frequently displayed the coffin in the theater lobby until the final night of his engagement, when it was brought onto the stage so he could perform his escape. But despite such measures to attract crowds, business began falling off badly during the political upheavals near the close of King Alfonso's reign in the late 1920s.

In one town, shooting broke out during Raymond's performance and the audience fled from the theater while police were rounding up members of the rival factions. The trouble centered around a local politician named Hierro, who had apparently ducked out during the fray, because nobody could find him. As a result, the police gave up their search and released the suspects who had been seeking Hierro as their target.

Meanwhile, Raymond had canceled the rest of the engagement, knowing that there would be no more business. The stage crew was packing up, hoping to make the train to the next town, when somebody remembered the coffin in the lobby. Since it was standing upright, with the lid closed, like a door, they tilted it to carry it to the truck.

As they did so, the lid flipped open and out rolled the body of Hierro. That was where his rivals had hurriedly hidden the victim, to clear themselves with the police. The empty coffin was packed with the rest of Raymond's equipment, but he didn't stop at the next town. He kept on to the next country, Portugal.

From Portugal, Raymond returned to South America, to repeat his triumphs of a dozen years before. Elbert Hubbard had whimsically suggested that Raymond should go forth to all lands as the "King of America." That belonged to a forgotten era, but now, Spanish speaking audiences began playing upon the words *rey* and *mundo*, meaning "king" and "world." Where magic was concerned, Raymond was indeed "King of the World."

Among the many specialty performers with Raymond's show was Litzka Gonser, a young American *harpiste* who had studied at the Royal Conservatory in Brussels and had played with the Boston Symphony and London Symphony orchestras. Litzka had been giving concerts in London when Raymond engaged her for the British and European tour. By the time the show reached Portugal, a romance had grown between them. Litzka continued on the world tour, and soon after their arrival in Montevideo, she and Raymond were married.

All through South America, Litzka's harp solos were a feature of the show, and she also performed in some of Raymond's principal illusions. In Lima, Peru, Raymond presented his version of the latest sensational illusion, "Sawing a Woman in Half." He called for two men to hold Litzka's head and feet while he did the sawing. The two volunteers who responded were the President of Peru and the United States Ambassador. Naturally, the audience liked that.

The audience liked Raymond, too, as did all his Latin-American audiences, northward through Ecuador, Colombia, Central America and Mexico. Finally, late in 1930, Raymond reached California. There he condensed the cream of his magic into a one-hour presentation and began a forty-week tour of the largest motion-picture houses from Los Angeles to New York and back.

For elegance and artistry, that show still stands unique. Seven magnificent curtains rose grandly, one by one, while a dozen girls in herald costumes stepped on from the wings in pairs, blowing fanfares on long trumpets. The last of the curtains disclosed an upright framework of glittering chrome at the top of a short flight of steps. Two girl dancers carrying lighted torches came onstage turning handsprings, and reached the skeleton cabinet just as the trumpets sounded a crescendo.

The dancers applied their torches to the framework, there was a puff of smoke and flame, and from it stepped the Great Raymond, immaculately attired in evening clothes. Beaming his most inscrutable smile, he descended the steps and approached the footlights. The trumpeters followed in a double column, playing a triumphal march; they divided into two lines which continued to the opposite wings, each followed by a torch-bearer.

By then, the audience was eager to witness Raymond's magic. He began by showing two empty glass bowls, placing each on an undraped table and covering it with a plain napkin. Moments later, the bowls were brimming with dozens of real oranges, which he tossed to the audience.

So natural was the procedure that the effect seemed sheer magic. This also applied to Raymond's startling productions of pigeons and ducks, while still greater marvels followed. A cabinet was shown empty and its front covered with a paper frame; a moving shadow which appeared there materialized into a living person who broke through the paper. A girl was seated in a chair which was raised by ropes above the stage; a pistol shot, a puff of smoke, and the chair fell to the stage empty, for the girl was completely gone!

Raymond's consummate skill was at its best when he transformed strips of colored tissue paper into a Chinese hat. He did the entire routine with one hand only, to the accompaniment of tinkly Oriental music, before a costly Chinese curtain, which was used in that trick alone. A girl then stepped onstage wearing a special Chinese costume, to be crowned with the paper hat and take a bow with the magician.

The show finished with the "Trunk Trick," now known as "Metempsychosis," and still as startling a mystery as when Raymond had termed it "The Flight of Satteka." It left people not only wondering, but watching for Raymond's return, so they could witness the marvel again. But Raymond decided that one such tour was enough. The schedule of four and five shows a day demanded by the big movie houses was too grueling, forcing both Raymond and his company to sacrifice artistry in favor of routine.

Besides, Raymond's zest for magic was sparked by the freedom and adventure that it offered. Those elements were missing on a "five-a-day circuit." So Raymond went back to his full evening show, presenting it under various auspices in theaters and auditoriums across the United States.

Raymond often divided the full show into two parts, each slightly longer than an hour, with fifteen minutes between. During a matinee in Los Angeles, when hundreds of children clamored for more magic during the intermission, Litzka made a surprise appearance in a Chinese costume and produced hat-loads of popcorn and candy, followed by a live rabbit.

The excitement brought Raymond from his dressing room to find his stage taken over by a Chinese wizard. Far from having misgivings over such a rivalry, he suggested that Litzka add more tricks to the routine. Gradually, it grew into a complete act of Chinese magic that Litzka presented as a regular feature of the Raymond show.

With each succeeding season, Raymond continued his over-all planning for another world tour, only to postpone it, time and again, due to the constantly increasing threat of World War II. By the time that conflict ended, Raymond was on the verge of retirement. On September 10, 1945, Raymond and Litzka put on their magic with a company of assistants at Town Hall in New York.

During the full evening show, an audience of magical connoisseurs watched Raymond perform classic effects of conjuring in his inimitable style. But the golden age of wizardry had returned for that night only. It was Raymond's farewell performance. His health was steadily declining and he was forced to abandon his contemplated tour, though Litzka continued to present her Chinese magic in vaudeville during those last few years.

On January 27, 1948, the magic world was saddened by the death of the man who had combined his art with adventure, as no one ever had before, and perhaps never will. With the passing of the Great Raymond, a great era of magic had also gone.

215

Maurer, Otto, 142
Mediums: Anderson and, 63; Davenport Brothers and, 90–91; Houdini and, 164–65, 184; Raymond and, 190, 192; Robinson and, 105, 124
Melville (Scotland Yard superintendent), 173
Mendoza, Argentina, 196–98
Mentalism. See Mind-reading acts
"Metamorphosis," 168, 173
"Metempsychosis," 212
Mexico, 92, 211
"Mid-air Vanish," 106–9, 113
"Milk Can Escape," 176–78, 183, 185
Milk churns, escape from, 180–81
Mind-reading acts, 105, 160, 192, 199. See also Mediums; "Second Sight"
Minneapolis, Minn., 172
"Miraculous Umbrella," 54
Mirrors, use of, 78–80, 152, 157
"Miser's Dream," 71, 88
Modern Magic (Hoffmann), 55–56, 132
Moody, Dwight, 134
"Moth and the Flame, The," 151–53
Municipal Theater (Lima, Peru), 207
"Mysteries of India," 159

Nana Sahib, 109
Naples, Italy, 9, 10
Napoleon Bonaparte, 66
Natural Magic (Astley), 48
Neveu, Colonel de, 40, 41, 42
New York City: Anderson in, 63; Ching Ling Foo in, 110; Herrmann in, 69, 70, 84; Houdini in, 162–66, 168–69, 184; Robinson in, 110–12; Thurston in, 133–34, 141–45
New York State, 213, 217. See also specific cities
"Night in Japan, A," 85
"Night in the Palace of Peking, A," (extravaganza), 19
"Noah's Ark," 80–81, 85, 201
Norfolk, Va., 182
Noriet (watchmaker), 4
Nova Scotia, 170–71

Oakland, Calif., 183
"Obedient Cards," 23
"Omelet Trick," 12–14
Oranges, vanishing, 82–83
Orange tree trick, 9, 23
"Organ Pipes," 192–93

Oriental magic, 201–5. See also Chinese tricks; Hindu magic; specific acts, magicians
Orpheum vaudeville circuit, 172, 173, 183
"Overboard Box Excape," 185
Ozanam (writer on magic), 2

Packing cases, escape from, 170, 185
Palace Theatre (London), 145
Palais des Prestiges (Paris theater), 18–20
Palais Royal, 22, 29, 30, 38, 39
"Palanquin Production," 113, 156
"Paligenisia," 162, 184
Palming, 3, 142–43. See also Cards and card tricks; Sleights of hand
Panama, 207
Panmure, Lord, 50
Pantage circuit, 183–84
Paris, France: Herrmann in, 66, 68, 83; Raymond in, 207, 208; Robert-Houdin in, 15, 16, 19, 20, 27, 29, 38; Robinson in, 113–16
Pastor, Tony, vaudeville house of, 143, 149, 161
"Pastry Cook of the Palais Royal" (mechanical trick), 23
Path, Olive ("Dot"; Suee Seen), 105–9, 111, 113, 115–23, 127–29
Pedro II (Dom Pedro), Emperor of Brazil, 92
Peru, 207, 211
"Phantom Supper," 192–93
Philadelphia, Pa., 92, 131, 134
Philippe (Jacques Noël Talon), 18–20, 35–36
Philistine, The (magazine), 206
"Phoenixsistography," 52
Picks, handcuff escapes and use of, 176, 196
"Pigeon Catching," 199
Pigeons, tricks using, 19–20, 53–54, 132, 146, 199, 212
Pinetti, Chevalier, 9–10, 25, 168
"Piquet Trick" (card trick), 7, 14
Pistols. See Bullet-catching trick
Pond, Major James B., 189–90
Portfolio, magic, 47, 58–59, 61
Portugal, 67, 200, 210, 211
Posters, advertising, x–xiii, 59–60
Prado, Don Mariano del, 68
Prestidigitation, origin of term, 17–18, 20

ABOUT THE AUTHOR

An amateur magician himself, Walter Gibson has been interested in magic for most of his life. He has written eighteen books and numerous articles on the subject, has edited four magic magazines, and has known personally the greatest magicians of the past fifty years. He traveled, worked, and wrote with Thurston, Blackstone, Houdini, and Raymond and from them gained first-hand impressions of an earlier generation of magicians. In the course of his active career, he also wrote the famous "Shadow" novels, under the pen name of Maxwell Grant. Mr. Gibson lives in Putnam Valley, New York, with his wife, Litzka (formerly Mrs. Raymond), who is a writer, harpist, and magician.